I've travelled the world twice over,
Met the famous: saints and sinners,
Poets and artists, kings and queens,
Old stars and hopeful beginners,
I've been where no-one's been before,
Learned secrets from writers and cooks
All with one library ticket
To the wonderful world of books.

© JANICE JAMES.

HURRICANE
OVER THE JUNGLE

On 30th October 1941, No. 258 Squadron left Scotland for Singapore, Sumatra and Java. In the next 120 days the 22 pilots were reduced to a handful. Those who had not been killed had become prisoners of the Japanese. The author, who was one of the pilots, recounts the events of those days. He recaptures the atmosphere of the bitter aerial engagements, of the hostile jungle terrain over which they were battling, and movingly recalls what it was like to see his comrades dying one by one.

Books by Terence Kelly
in the Ulverscroft Large Print Series:

LONG LIVE THE SPY
THE SPY IS DEAD
VOYAGE BEYOND BELIEF

TERENCE KELLY

HURRICANE OVER THE JUNGLE

Complete and Unabridged

ULVERSCROFT
Leicester

First published in Great Britain in 1977

First Large Print Edition
published August 1993

British Library CIP Data

Kelly, Terence
Hurricane over the jungle.—Large print ed.—
Ulverscroft large print series: non-fiction
I. Title
940.5425092

ISBN 0–7089–2913–3

Published by
F. A. Thorpe (Publishing) Ltd.
Anstey, Leicestershire

Set by Words & Graphics Ltd.
Anstey, Leicestershire
Printed and bound in Great Britain by
T. J. Press (Padstow) Ltd., Padstow, Cornwall

This book is printed on acid-free paper

To the memory of my brother, Desmond, who was killed when the Lancaster of which he was Observer, was shot down over Holland on his birthday, June 21st, 1943; to the pilots of 258 Squadron whether living or dead with grateful thanks for those who provided photographic and other material for this book; to the pilots of those other Squadrons who played at least as active a part in the events recounted and particularly to those 232, 488 and 605 Squadrons; to the ground staffs of all Squadrons (including those of 242) who took part in Singapore, Sumatra and Java, of whom not a few were killed or wounded and the majority taken prisoner by the Japanese.

Acknowledgement of Quotations

These occur on the pages listed. They are all taken from Churchill's *The Second World War* published by Cassell

page 1 from p 493 of Volume Three
page 63 from p 87 of Volume Four
page 74 from pp 87 & 88 of Volume Four
page 79 from pp 85 & 86 of Volume Four
page 147 from p 123 of Volume Four

Foreword by
Marshal of the Royal Air Force,
Sir Denis Spotswood,
GCB, CBE, DSO, DFC

It is more likely than otherwise that most people in this year of grace 1977 will have gained their knowledge of the events of 1939 – 1945 through history books or the records of great figures. As a result, the majority may well lack insight into 'what went on' as seen and felt by those in junior positions who were in physical contact with the enemy.

Terence Kelly describes his book as an attempt to fill in 120 days in the life of a squadron when formal records of that life could not be kept. I suggest that it is more than this. It is a worthwhile outline of a junior fighter pilot's attempt to come to terms with an unbrilliant period of British and Allied history. I refer to the loss of Singapore and subsequently that of the Dutch East Indies. He is critical of organisation, morale and equipment (or lack of them) as he saw them in the theatre of which he writes; and I, for one, would not question his criticism.

However, I suggest that it needs to be borne in mind that Great Britain had stood virtually alone for some two years against Germany and Italy; and the entry of Japan also into the war against us could have almost come into the category, for many of those directly involved, of the straw and the camel's back. This is not to excuse but to provide perspective.

What is more important, I suggest also, is that our situation was brought about, as much as by anything else, by the locust years of the 1920's and 1930's when those who warned us about our prospective enemies were ignored — the 'ten year rule' and the like. We had ourselves to blame, therefore, in large measure for the shortcomings to which Terence Kelly draws attention and which caused then, and continue to cause, such havoc in our affairs. Indeed, some may well argue that those locust years (in Great Britain and other countries) were as much the cause as any of World War II itself.

I share the opinion of many in all walks who see the grave risk of a repetition in our affairs if we continue to avoid our national responsibilities for defence — whatever specious arguments are put forward to justify defence cuts; and they are specious.

Terence Kelly, then a young fighter pilot, with more than enough to keep himself occupied in extraordinarily difficult circumstances shows an acute power of observation to be put to good use later in his career as playwright and author. He is the first to admit that there can be gaps in his memory after some thirty-five years. But, nevertheless, his personal record is extremely interesting and well worth reading, not only for the content of the book. This, as I have suggested, is useful in reminding all of us that war is much a matter of individuals; and that we ignore our defences at our peril.

Preface

Every Royal Air Force Squadron has its diary which is kept in the Public Records Office behind the Law Courts in London. Here every flight, every triumph, every accident, every death, even every leave and visit to sick bay by its pilots is put down often with wry, droll, even facetious comments. The squadron essence is there, changing as pilots come and go, changing with the personality of the commanding officers who come and go as well, changing with the War's demands. These diaries, which all may read, are chronicles of small groups of young men who came together to fly and to share a unique style of companionship before through promotion, posting, capture or death they went their separate ways. But the squadron, as a rule, went on, surviving disasters, absorbing its losses, rebuilding all the time. A squadron was a living entity greater and more durable than its parts and its diary was an uninterrupted history of its being.

As a rule.

But occasionally, exceptionally, the reader may find a break in the diary, a gap for which there is no explanation. No one in the Public Records Office can help him now; for a space the squadron has historically ceased to exist. When its life begins again new names appear, old names have been forgotten, and, possibly, a few of those which have become familiar bridge the gap.

Such a squadron was 258 Fighter Squadron Royal Air Force.

On October 30th 1941, twenty-two pilots of very mixed nationalities — American, Australian, Canadian, English, Irish, Rhodesian, Scottish and New Zealand — left Scotland for a then unknown destination and in the records the names of these twenty-two are listed.

The next entry is in Ceylon 120 days later when a new officer takes command. The records show a mere handful of the original 22.

What happened in those 120 days is told in the pages which follow, as seen through the eyes of one of the twenty-two.

It is a small piece of history.

On October 3rd 1941, No 258 Squadron flew its Hurricanes from Martlesham Heath to Debden, shooting (as the official records say) 'a terrific line by flying in formation in the shape of an arrow ... seventeen aircraft thrusting their way to rout all in front of them!' And that night there was a 'terrific party in the Sergeant's Mess' in which for some reason long since forgotten the seventeen pilots linked arms and equally routed all and sundry from their path. Through the following days five new pilots were posted to them and then all were sent on a long leave which was abruptly terminated so that it was possible to record in the Operational Records Book for October 30th the following:

Early calls at 05.30 were a grim necessity as some of the tropical kit had not yet come and was expected in the early hours. The kit did not arrive until 06.45 hours and a fantastic clothing parade was held in the Ladies' Room of the Officers Mess. The kit was hastily issued and with no more ado the twenty-two pilots left for Scotland with their 90 lbs of kit each. The party was as follows:

S/L J. A. Thomson, Flt/Lt D. J. T. Sharp, Flt/Lt V. B. de la Perelle, F/O A. G. Donahue, F/O Dobbyn, P/O A. H. Milnes, P/O McAlister, P/O White, P/O Geffene, P/O Macnamara, P/O A. D. M. Nash, P/O McCulloch, P/O C. Kleckner, P/O J. A. Campbell, Sgt Keedwell, Sgt Kelly, Sgt Nicholls, Sgt Lambert, Sgt Healey, Sgt Sheerin, Sgt Glynn, Sgt Scott.

There are no more entries in the Record Book until March 1st 1942. The entry for that date reads:

On this date Squadron had the designation 'K' Squadron. Acting Squadron Leader P. C. Fletcher assumed command w.e.f. 28.2.42. On this date 5 Senior NCOs and

25 airmen had been posted to the Squadron.

The entry for March 7th reads:

Flt/Lt D. J. T. Sharp, P/O Macnamara, P/O N. L. McCulloch, P/O A. H. Milnes, P/O C. G. White, P/O D. B. F. Nicholls posted to Squadron for flying duties.

On March 30th the Squadron was given the designation 258 Squadron (it was found that a fair proportion of personnel were on the strength of the original 258 Squadron disbanded in Sumatra).'

On April 5th the Japanese attacked Colombo Harbour.

The Operational Record Book states:

The nine Hurricane IIs scrambled as a Squadron and the five Hurricane Is as an independent flight. One or two enemy aircraft were encountered overhead but the main body, approximately 75 enemy aircraft were then concentrated over the harbour with approximately 35 Navy 0s a few thousand feet above acting as cover. As 258 Squadron approached the Harbour the enemy bombers were preparing to attack. When the Squadron arrived in the harbour it was on a level with the enemy bombers and below the Navy 0s. Squadron Leader Fletcher attacked the bombers with the Hurricane IIs. He continued to attack for as long a period as possible.

Of the fourteen Hurricanes involved in this affair, nine were shot down with five pilots killed and two injured. None of those killed or injured were of the original 258 Squadron which fact bears testimony to the experience gained in the account which follows.

On April 13th Pilot Officer Nash and Sergeant Scott arrived to rejoin the squadron and on April 18th, Flying Officer Donahue.

Thus of the original twenty-two pilots, nine remained; of the balance eleven were either prisoner of war or dead. Of these nine only three remained in the Air Force List at the conclusion of hostilities.

The only pilots who appear to have escaped either death, or imprisonment by the Japanese, were: Thomson, Sharp, White, Milnes, McCulloch, Nicholls and Sheerin.

Number 258 Squadron R.A.F.

List of pilots in Squadron Operational Records Book on October 30th 1941. N.B. Other pilots were later attached of whom mention is made later.

Name	*Nationality*
S/L J. A. Thomson Survived War	British
Flt/Lt D. J. T Sharp Survived War	New Zealander
Flt/Lt V. B. de la Perelle P. O. W. Japan	New Zealander
F/O A. G. Donahue Killed in Action after leaving 258 Squadron	American
F/O H. A. Dobbyn Killed in Action with 258 Squadron	New Zealander
P/O A. H. Milnes Survived War	British

P/O B. McAlister Killed in Action with 258 Squadron	New Zealander
P/O C. Campbell-White Survived War	New Zealander
P/O D. Geffene Killed in Action with 258 Squadron	American
P/O G. C. S. Macnamara Died after War of wounds received in action	Rhodesian
P/O A. D. M. Nash Killed in Flying Accident	British
P/O N. L. McCulloch Survived War	British
P/O C. Kleckner Killed in Action with 258 Squadron	American
P/O J. A. Campbell P. O. W. Japan	American
Sgt R. B. Keedwell Died from burns with 258 Squadron	Canadian
Sgt C. T. R. Kelly P. O. W. Japan	British
Sgt D. B. F. Nicholls Survived War	British

Sgt A. Lambert P. O. W. Japan	British
Sgt P. R. T. Healey P. O. W. Japan	Australian
Sgt A. Sheerin Survived War	British
Sgt K. Glynn Killed in Action with 258 Squadron	Canadian
Sgt N. M. Scott Killed in Flying Accident	Canadian

1

Ripples of a sinking
— and the outbreak of a war

OF the sinking of the *Ark Royal*, Winston Churchill wrote:

On November 12th (1941) while returning from Gibraltar after flying more aircraft into Malta, the *Ark Royal* was struck by a torpedo from a German U-boat. All attempts to save the ship failed, and this famous veteran which had played such a distinguished part in our affairs sank when only twenty five miles from Gibraltar.

The ripples from that sinking must have spread very far but perhaps apart from those on the ship itself, on which there was but one casualty, there were few more immediately affected than the pilots of 258 Squadron.

Theoretically 258 was a New Zealand

squadron but by time it had been much adulterated. There had been two Indians, Pujji and Latif, three Poles, Paderewski, Stabrowski and Zbierchowski, two Czechs, Franczak and Kropiwnicki and two more, Sodek and Sticka, who usually flew together; one of them who was the Section Leader was forever bellowing through his intercom to his Number Two to come in closer — until one day he bellowed to such effect that he found his compatriot's wingtip keeping him company in his cockpit and then there were two less Hurricanes and two angry Czechs floating down on Purley in that wonderful summer's sunshine. And again there had been a French Canadian called Hank Duval who had been shot down in July during a fighter sweep escorting bombers on an attack on Potez aircraft factory, had promptly escaped to Spain and managing to get back home within the month was snatched from the squadron by Intelligence.

They had come and gone, men of many nationalities, in and out of this pot pourri of a squadron which now found itself by one of the myriad accidents of war marooned in the weary inactivity of Gibraltar.

It should have been the briefest pause. On November 1st 1941 HMS *Athene*, a ship designed to carry aircraft yet not an aircraft carrier, sailed from Abbotsinch near Glasgow in company with aircraft carrier *Hermes*. The combined complement of Hurricanes and pilots was seventy-two: three squadrons. Their machines were not the normal eight or twelve machine gun Hurricanes but carried four cannons and were fitted with long range tanks. The cannon were for tank busting in Operation Crusader intended to sweep Rommel from Cyrenaica, and by November 21st when *Athene* docked by the Gibraltar mole, the battle was already joined; the long range tanks were required for the long sea haul. The plan was two staged, the first of these to be achieved by flying the aircraft in two batches off the flight deck of *Ark Royal* at a Point 'X' in the Mediterranean six hundred miles west of Malta to Luqa aerodrome, the second by the seventy-two escorted by a Blenheim or two flying from Luqa to Alexandria.

The three squadrons were Nos 242, 258 and 605. Coins were spun and half of 605 and the whole of 242 embarked and in due course took off for Luqa, only 34 of the 36 arriving; the missing two had presumably run out of fuel and thus thrown doubt on the validity of the entire operation. Meanwhile 258 and the balance of 605 waited in Gibraltar.

I cannot but believe that the sinking of *Ark Royal* saved the lives of quite a number of pilots who were to survive the war. The distance from Malta to Alexandria is, in rough terms, 900 miles and the route for most of the first 650 lay within 200, and at times 60, miles of territory then occupied by the Axis forces. There was risk from Sicily, Libya, Greece and Crete apart from the added, although admittedly slighter, danger of carrier borne aircraft. The normal range of the Hurricane Mark 11B fitted with its usual armament was 480 miles, a range which would decrease when the aircraft was flown in any sort of formation and for the rearmost aircraft when the formation was a large one, quite dramatically. With long range tanks the range was theoretically increased to 985 miles and the idea was to have the Hurricanes, rendered cumbersome and unwieldy by the extra weight and drag of the cannons and long range tanks, creep through the sky, hanging almost as it were by sky hooks for fifty-five minutes of each hour and then for the other five for the throttles to be opened up to burn the deposit off the plugs.

At the time the idea was conceived, with the exception of the 70th British Division beleagured in Tobruk, the whole of Libya was in German hands with Sollum held by them as an Egyptian outpost. At the time when the projected flight would have taken place a fierce battle was raging in the desert, and such aircraft as the Germans could spare from the Russian front were much on the alert. The shortest landfall once the point of no return from Malta had been passed would have been at about Sidi Barrani — assuming that with no one to guide him the pilot would have been able to find it before his tanks ran dry — and even this, with the Egyptian coastline running away from the direct Malta to

Alexandria route, would have been only marginally nearer. And had the wind become suddenly adverse or there been the most modest of intervention by the Luftwaffe the whole project would have ended in total disaster.

But the *Ark Royal* was sunk and so it wasn't in the long run tried; the thirty-four in Malta stayed there and the thirty-six still in Gibraltar waited.

There are a large number of places in the world where to have nothing much to do is wearisome and Gibraltar in December of 1941 was one of these and probably for the sergeant pilots it was marginally more tedious than for the officers. There were eight sergeant pilots, of which I was one, the others being two Canadians named Keedwell and Scott, an Australian, Sheerin and four English, Nicholls, Lambert, Healey and Glynn who being believed to be the youngest in the squadron was nicknamed 'Junior'. In fact at the time the 258 complement was under strength and there were only fourteen officers of which five, Sharp, de la Perelle, Dobbyn, McAlister and White were

New Zealanders, four, Donahue, Geffene, Kleckner and Campbell were Americans, one, Macnamara, a Rhodesian, one McCulloch, a Scot and the balance Thomson, the Commanding Officer new to the squadron, Milnes and Nash were English.

There was of course a degree of distinction between sergeants and officers but it wasn't very deep on leaves or active service with many of the closest friendships clear across the line. On the *Athene* and in Gibraltar it was more defined; Naval attitudes were violently opposed to mingling aboard ship and in Gibraltar all the few places of quality were out of bounds to other ranks. It was almost as irritating to officers as to sergeants; of the officers — American and Rhodesian pilots were automatically commissioned — at least four McAlister, Dobbyn, White and McCulloch were only lately commissioned and of the sergeants all who were not killed or taken prisoner were commissioned later. Various stratagems were employed such as fake 'tactics meetings' in the Wardroom or cabins so that afloat the sergeants could at least have more to drink than their tot of rum, and in fact there was on the later trip on *Athene* what was really quite a disgraceful battle between RAF and Navy in the course of which if memory serves me correctly Jimmy the One's trousers ended up flying from the mast.

Ashore the situation was in its way perhaps even more curious still for there were no regulations against the officers and other ranks fraternising — only about the places they might frequent. But the bars and brothels of La Linea and Algeciras knew of course nothing of such nonsense and became almost by force majeure the regular meeting grounds.

Perhaps amongst the officers the one who objected most was Campbell, nicknamed 'Red' because of the flaming colour of his hair and rather a Mickey Rooney sort of fellow except that he was bigger. Campbell, one of the Americans, probably after Nash the youngest officer, nineteen or so, thought the whole thing utter nonsense and it was not surprising that he should be the one to announce the end of tedium on a lump of rock with a single street of consequence, a cinema, a tea place and a handful of rough and tumble bars.

He came roaring into the iron clad box where we sergeants, eight of us, who slept like a row of suspended bananas in a line of hammocks, were killing time on the Sunday afternoon of December 7th, playing cards, reading or letterwriting, to announce with glee the stunning news that the United States was in the war at last and enthusiasm being the stuff of youth the reaction to his obvious jubilation was an equal exhilaration.

And what were they like, these other seven sergeants crowding round Red Campbell listening to the news of Pearl Harbor, of whom only two were not to be killed or taken prisoner?

There was Bertie Lambert who came from Middlesbrough, tiny and neat with a baby face, a parroty sort of nose and smooth hair always shining from Vaseline Hair Tonic and with a fund of personal expressions which became squadron sayings. There was 'Pip' Healey, intelligent, rather tall with sad eyes set deep into brownish caverns,

'Nicky' Nicholls with quiet ways, reserved, a little more difficult to know and Kenneth Glynn whose father was a Commander of some ship — 'Junior' with very clean, ingenuous looks and an engaging diffidence. There were the two Canadians, very contrasting — Scott called 'Scotty', big, loose and husky who could well have been a logger, and Roy Keedwell compact, relaxed, with an attractive voice and rather secret eyes and a smile always just hovering on his lips. And there was 'Arty' Sheerin with a very long and weatherbeaten Australian face, an uncomplicated chap.

And there was me. I'd got there accidentally. I had a brother whose ambition had always been to fly. He joined the RAFVR before the war but couldn't pass his flying test; when the war broke out being on the reserve he was called up at once and was firmly on the ground until his two years younger brother became a pilot when he remustered as observer, sadly to be killed on a very early Op on his twenty-third birthday.

I had no ambitions to fly; it never

crossed my mind. In fact I had no particular ambition to being in the services at all but finally gave up taking professional examinations when I found myself with, practically speaking, nothing but girls for company. I ambled along to the RAF recruiting centre with nothing particularly in mind and when the Recruiting Officer suggested I put myself down as pilot I did so with a certain apprehension fortunately tempered by the conviction I hadn't a cat in hell's chance of passing the then stringent medical tests and if I did that I'd even more certainly fail the flying ones. But I ended up a Hurricane pilot, very proud of my brevet, very surprised at what had happened and still a little puzzled as to how the damn thing kept up anyway.

2

From the Gold Coast to the Nile

ON Christmas Eve the *Athene* sailed away from Gibraltar, alone and unescorted. The weary days enlivened only by endless patrols on Catalina flying boats when passing Focke Wolfe Condors on identical reconnaissance missions for the other side were ships of the air to whom one waved in passing, the magical night long antisubmarine patrols on MTBs whose Naval captains had been gun runners for both sides in the Spanish Civil War, the sweet cakes in the café in the spine street of Gibraltar, the brothels of La Linea, the almonds in paper twists, the cinema, the raucous, garish bars and the boozy nights, the gimcrack souvenirs, the long, drunken lurch all round the harbour to the eight swinging hammocks side by side each twelve inches from its neighbour, the Andrews Sisters and 'I'll be with you in Apple Blossom Time', the clanging watertight door, the endless Spam bloodied by beetroot — all this was over, vague, insignificant, fading with the wake of *Athene* heading south, leaving only odd reflections which would root: the exit of Don Geffene, one of the two Californians, who, practising from the airport under the shadow of the rock had landed in Algeciras to be interned, later to escape and later still be shot down and killed on Easter Sunday by the Japanese; the failure of Junior, even in a brothel, to break his duck; the hairsbreadth salvation of Scotty from a Spanish gaol; the sickening thud of Bertie, looping the loop in his hammock and stalling at the top.

It was over — five weeks of stagnation was at an end.

I remember the magic of that week at sea, the magic of the first experience of sailing in tropical waters which has never been quite repeated; the old constellations sank and the new ones rose and the sea silvered by moon and starlight hissed fast along the hull. There were duties to perform: four hour shifts manning two of

Athene's pom-pom anti aircraft guns and night watches under the soft, warm, star powdered sky. There were incidents; the rebellion against rank discrimination, the stentorian yell by Kleckner: 'Submarine on the port bow' bringing the Captain in a bath towel needlessly on the bridge to view a passing log, the renewed 'tactics' cocktail parties . . .

On New Year's Eve, the *Athene* dropped anchor in Freetown Harbour and at once a pall of wet, suffocating heat fell on the ship and every metal surface dripped moisture while above a blazing sun burned from a metal sky. The mysteries of why ships stop and wait were unexplained, but a sea hose was rigged on deck and an awning was constructed. We writhed with dhobie itch and the sea was oil and the boredom broken only by the skinny natives in their bumboats paddling out. Two hundred yards away the town lay shabby — rusting roofs and heat and squalor. A single red track straggled glistening upwards into the steaming green of Africa, westwards through an infinity of distance which had never

14

been considered in Middlesbrough or Finchley.

At nightfall we were off again and it was still a tremendous mystery as the *Athene* shifted in calm seas and an eerie evenness still southwards with Hurricanes hawsered on its decks and the Southern Cross rising from the phosphorescent sea into the blazing starlit sky.

The next day we anchored at Takoradi in the Gold Coast and finally bade farewell to the faithful *Athene*, the goddess of wisdom, who kept the mystery of where she was going sealed within her bows — and on her decks where our Hurricanes, still hawsered, salt encrusted, stayed, as if they were to rust forever and never fly again. The *Athene* sailed away taking our Hurricanes and no one knew where she was going, nor ever heard where she had gone.

★ ★ ★

It was tremendous stuff. Perhaps it was the Irish in me which found a preposterous pleasure in what is to most discomfort. The higher the temperature, the thicker the mosquito swarms, the more romantic and satisfying Africa became. I didn't so much see the lizards on the walls or hear the bullfrogs in the night as new experiences but as proof positive I was in Africa. A voracious reader, I was aware of a powerful sense of *déjà vu* as I sat in the Sergeant's mess in Takoradi with the slow turning fans stirring the hot air like soup and native servants at my elbow. The spirits of Saki and Henty and Somerset Maugham hung over me effectively cutting off the past as if it had never been and making of the future exactly the total mystery of the red track of Freetown leading upwards through the green. As I had rested my arms gingerly on the burning rail, soaked with sweat, my crutch a torment of dhobie itch, my tan pith helmet harsh as a crown jammed down tight upon my head, staring at that red track which shone like steel after rain I hadn't seen it at all, as probably it was, a short lived road to some settlement behind the first green ridge, but as virginal, an entrance to the land of Zulus, Fuzzy Wuzzys, crocodiles and

16

cannibals; of slavers, pygmys, pythons; a land of dark, deep jungles where tigers crept and awesome spiders lurked.

The old world fell away from me, I knew a freedom quite unimaginable before.

On January 3rd 1942 we became passengers on a Douglas DC3. I even have the pilot's name, Captain Sherman, an American airlines' pilot, and the aircraft's number 25623 written in my log book. We flew inland from Takoradi then down to Accra and then Lagos for refuelling. We lunched in the dry burning heat in the walled city, Kano, strangely isolated in an empty desert; we spent the night in a private civilian club at Maidugeri near Lake Chad. On the following day we flew for six hours across the barren deserts of what was then French Equatorial Africa to lunch at a mosque-like building in El Fasher in the Sudan and by evening were driving through a swarm of insects from the airfield of Wadi Saidna to Khartoum.

These are small things now; they were big things then. It seemed the most exciting, remarkable trip imaginable. All was new to all and we had no idea where we were going. At every port of call, with the most tremendous urgency and organisation a fleet of cars or a pair of trucks would race out and formate on the aircraft even before it stopped as if each moment was vital. We would be whisked off with the least delay to waiting drinks and waiting meals. It all engendered a feeling of tremendous purpose. Clearly we had been selected for some dramatic exploit of enormous portent, far too secret to be disclosed but every moment vital. It was simply huge adventure — we were in our prime, a dismembered squadron become one again. There were no rules in the stripped out aircraft, no bounds, no frowning Naval officers.

It was odd but as far as I can remember where we were going didn't seem particularly important. I suppose we assumed it was to fly against the Japanese, but I wouldn't be sure of it. It was just a huge experience filled with zest, elation, excitement and each halt offering a different race, different architecture, food and atmosphere . . . and one stride more towards the answer to the mystery.

And then, in the end, the haste was shown as mere efficiency for once in Khartoum the sense of urgency was quite gone and in its place were pleasant easy days and romantic, convivial nights and beautiful hostesses in long, clinging, evening dresses on the roof gardens of the night clubs. The war seemed a splendid vehicle and no one was complaining; the only danger was that someone might bring it to an end.

★ ★ ★

A few of us went ahead of the main body to ferry Hurricanes at Port Sudan. It was a weird aircraft they used for transporting us, one of the three Vickers Wellesleys now possibly converted which jointly held the world long distance flying record — seven thousand one hundred and sixty two miles. And it was piloted by one of the pilots who made that record, a Sergeant Dixon. It was a long thin aircraft and we sat three in a line as in a racing skiff.

I did a lot of reflecting on that trip

which took nearly four hours. I remember
thinking that it must have taken a hell of
a long time to do that seven thousand
one hundred and sixty two miles staring
at the whacking great radial engine up
in front, listening to its drone, aware
that it only needed a plug to start
spitting and you were sunk — sunk
without trace in the Indian Ocean or
wherever. They must have got jolly tired,
I thought, flying all those hours. It was
bad enough in a Hurricane doing convoy
patrols up and down the Norfolk coast
from Martlesham Heath. You got sleepy
doing that; even when you turned the
oxygen full on you nodded off. Nodded
off and when you came to found you
were heading down towards the drink
not a thousand feet below. So you yanked
back the stick and told yourself not to
be a bloody fool — a thousand feet
wasn't much to play with. And blow
me down, ten minutes later you were
off again. And I wondered idly if that
was the way Phillips had gone with the
first squadron I had been in, 3 Squadron.
Or George Allenby in 258. George had
been a friend of mine. We used to sing

a song cribbed from a popular dance tune of the time: 'And be like Georgie Washington who never told a lie' — only we'd substitute Georgie Allenby. So far as I know what happened to George never was discovered; he'd been flying Number Two to Bruce McAlister and they'd gone into cloud together and when Bruce came out, George had vanished.

I don't know why I should remember so clearly thinking all these things on that long trip; perhaps I wrote home about them. I came back to the Wellesley and wondered about that seven thousand miles, concluded it must have been specially equipped with three sets of controls. Three men in a boat. A pity, I thought, there weren't three sets now, then I could fly her and that would be quite a line in the log book. Second Pilot — Self. And the hours would count. Go up from two hundred and ninety two hours and twenty minutes solo to about two ninety six. And if I chucked in my six and a quarter night flying — only birds and fools fly and birds don't fly at night — chuck in that and I'd have my three hundred up. And then there was the eleven and a half on the Cat in Gib. One of the short trips but what a bore it had been. And they did it all the time! Forty-two hours non stop often enough. And the Focke Wulfs just the same. God what a life! As for that seven thousand miles in this old crate. Must have been bloody cold. You wouldn't know it was sizzling hot down there. Down by the Nile . . . but it wasn't the Nile any more. It was a railway. Must have turned east at Atbara. Difficult to tell out here with the sun right overhead. Well if we'd turned east we must be damn near halfway. And about time too. It could be a boring business flying. And funny how it took you, where it took you. Whole thing was funny. You go to a recruiting centre looking for a cosy billet and end up a pilot! Go to a squadron enjoying a nice peaceful summer patrolling North Sea convoys and find yourself the one pilot posted to another which spent the summer doing moderately risky things like fighter sweeps over France; run out of petrol and seeing a nice big field wave Denny Sharp goodbye and you should be so lucky it's not a field at all but West

Malling aerodrome and it's strawberries and cream and boring everyone because you've seen your first 109s; and now while most of them are still swanning around Khartoum you're in this amazing kite over a lot of nothing but a railway. Extraordinary thing the war when you come to think of it — all manner of people telling you to go to different places in the world and forgetting or neglecting to tell you why!

★ ★ ★

It is curious how amongst the loss of possessions remnants remain. In the hectic weeks in Singapore, Sumatra and Java before I was taken prisoner I was continually having to rekit myself to make up for the loss of a previous collection left behind in a hasty withdrawal exercise and by the time I was booted into Boei Glodok gaol in what was then Batavia the only original items remaining were my log book protecting two or three good sized squadron photographs and a wallet tooled with Egyptian hieroglyphics which contained amongst a few other odd items, all to become very precious, a letter in green ink written by a girl I'd met very briefly and had taken rowing in Torbay and a photograph of another who meant a good deal more but had, I was to discover ruefully in Sydney on my release from Japan, married a few months earlier. There was also a very small snapshot, which I must have taken as I wasn't on it, of others who had been ferried in the same or other Wellesleys to Port Sudan.

The background was a tent pitched in the sand in which, presumably, we slept and the group of half a dozen consisted of Ken Glynn ('Junior'), Bertie Lambert looking very diminutive, a big chap whose name regretfully I forget, Arthur Sheerin managing to look Australian, Roy Keedwell with his attractive smile and Scott, the only one without a pith helmet worn at a rakish angle, with his lopsided grin conveying the impression he normally conveyed, and usually not without justification, of not having quite recovered from yesterday's hangover.

So it does look rather as if it was the sergeants who had been picked on for the job in hand leaving the girls of Khartoum night clubs to be cared for almost solely by the officers.

Port Sudan was a God forsaken place, consisting as I recall it solely of two squares of arcaded buildings with a few shops, plonked down in the desert, a hotel out of bounds to us, some salt lakes where I fruitlessly tried my hand at barracuda fishing, and docks and airfield interconnected by a road built up from the desert by sand embankments with telegraph poles staggered on either side. All this was relevant, for the job was ferrying Hurricanes (of a wingspan wider than the distance between the poles had they been directly opposite each other) from the airfield down to the docks where they would be loaded on HMS *Indomitable*, a brand new aircraft carrier about to make her maiden operational trip.

The difficulty about taxying Hurricanes is twofold: firstly their angle of repose is such that the nose rears up and you can see nothing at all ahead and secondly that directional control is by the rudder which responds proportionately to the amount of slipstream affecting it. In other words the faster you taxi, the more control you have. There was about a mile of curving road, a large number of Hurricanes to be delivered and the telegraph poles were spaced about fifty yards apart. And it was very, very hot.

I remember someone commenting about it afterwards in something of this vein:

'Have to stick your head out one side, then the other, crabbing along, using your rudder and a blip of throttle as a steering wheel. Underdo it and you take the wingtip off and knock down all the bloody communications; overdo it and you end up in the desert on your nose! What a game!

'All right, let's have a go. Turn on the road. Open the throttle. No so much you arse!! — well not yet anyway, not till you've got the hang of it. Right. Here it comes. The first of the bloody Mohicans. Blip the throttle, full right rudder. Christ you're going to hit it! The first bloody one! Well what are you going to do? If you do nothing you'll hit it; if you jam on the brakes you'll be on your nose in the middle of the road. Holding up the traffic! Only one thing to do, open the throttle wide and pray! Missed it! Christ! By two bloody inches and a lick of paint. Okay. Bang on left rudder and stick your head out the other side.

'Oh, Christ, the road's got a bend as well! Here it comes. Don't give you much time do they? Miss one and then get straight and there's another one ready for you on the other side. Okay, more left rudder, lots of throttle and what the hell. Missed that too! Hooray, hoo bloody ray! Only about thirty three more each side! Join the Air Force and drive a Hurricane along a slalom in the middle of the desert! Here comes number two to port. Port, why not! Ship of the desert that's what I bloody well am. Might as well have joined the Navy! Or the Tank Corps! Missed you, you bugger! Right — come on four, we're getting the hang of it, getting the swing. That's the secret, keep it swinging, a nice steady S along the road. Of course we're bound to boil before we're done in any case. At S for snaky! Snaky, that's it . . . snakes alive, number five. Blimey! Did you feel that? Must have put one wheel in the sand!

Charlie you're talking to yourself! You're always talking to yourself. Who cares! In a fix, number six. It'll be heaven, number seven; don't be late for number eight. What a swine, number nine; what the gen? Number ten! . . . I know, I know, I know: it'll be 'still alive sixty five,' then '*Clickety Clix, Sixty Six!*'

— It really was quite a job. Digressing, that story reminds me of another — I had to go to Uxbridge to volunteer to join the RAF. I became one of a long queue inching along one side of a gloomy corridor, a queue which hardly seemed to vary in length at all in that as one man left it to enter the interviewing room another joined it from the world outside. On the opposite side of the corridor was another queue which hardly seemed to vary either — but the difference was it consisted of two men. The man in front of me in my queue was a restive sort of fellow who kept casting envious eyes on the two across the way. At length he asked a question of a passing orderly and then crossed the corridor and became a third man to the smaller queue. Within ten minutes he had been interviewed and accepted.

'Okay?' I called.

'OKAY!' he shouted back.

'What are you doing?' I asked.

'What d'you think?' he shouts. 'Not hanging around all day to join the RAF. I'm in the Navy!'

One wonders on the effect of that.

3

Across the Indies to Singapore

ON January 9th 1942 HMS *Indomitable* with John Morse in command weighed anchor from Port Sudan to set off southwards down the Red Sea carrying in addition to her own crews and aircraft 48 pilots and Hurricane IIs which were to fly off her deck at some new point 'X' for some new destination which had yet to be disclosed; half of the pilots were of 258 Squadron, the other half of 232.

It is necessary to pause and explain what later might otherwise seem an error for in fact 232 Squadron would, long before the *Indomitable* had reached Point X, be operating in Singapore.

On November 11th 1941, the ground staff of 232 Squadron and the ground staffs of each of Numbers 17, 135 and 136 Squadrons all equipped with Hurricane 11b's had sailed from Liverpool in a large convoy for a destination as yet unannounced but obviously the Middle East because of the equipment issued. Of the pilots of these four squadrons only six of each sailed with the crews, the balance remaining in England to follow later. By the time the convoy had reached Durban the Far East war had broken out and the decision was taken that 232 Squadron should be detached from the Wing of four squadrons and the six pilots of each of the other squadrons actually in the convoy posted to it. Thus a full squadron with 24 pilots and, in fact, 51 Hurricanes allocated to it could be sent by sea with all possible speed to Singapore. This smaller convoy sailed from Durban on December 24th, arriving in Singapore on January 13th, to be saved from destruction in a most determined bombing attack on approaching harbour only by a fierce tropical storm. By January 19th, the squadron was in action operating from the two airfields of Seletar and Kallang.

Meanwhile the balance, nineteen pilots, had left Ouston, where they had been stationed, for Padgate and thence Greenock from whence, on December 7th, they had sailed on a troopship arriving at Freetown on December 23rd and at Takoradi on December 29th (with the exception of the Commanding Officer, Squadron Leader Llewellin and a Flight Commander, Flight Lieutenant Julien who had flown on ahead to Khartoum and thence to Cairo). They were thus just two days ahead of 258 Squadron and had travelled in the same manner by Pan American to Khartoum and, subsequently, Port Sudan, having from various sources picked up, as did 258 Squadron, the odd pilots necessary to make their numbers up to squadron strength of 24.

The fortunes of these two squadrons were henceforth to be interwoven although each largely retained its identity; there was a degree of intermingling socially, yet never at any time a sense of integration and little more than passing interest in each other's exploits.

Indomitable was quite a different kettle of fish from *Athene*. The was naturally a degree of segregation between sergeants and officers, but the gulf in quality of sleeping quarters much diminished. One could sling a hammock anywhere and in fact after a day or two I abandoned mine altogether and took to sleeping on a kind of shelf I discovered on the port side of the edge of the *Indomitable*, and being able to lie and hear the gentle hiss of a quiet sea a hundred feet below and watch the stars swinging in the sky I envied no one. It would be absurd to suggest I would not have preferred to be commissioned but it was only a question of time and patience. In any case I only had my own obstinacy to blame. I had been educated at a public school with Officers Training Corps against which I took an initial, never to be removed, objection following from the induction on my first day at school by a Sergeant Major who pronounced that membership of the OTC was compulsory and it followed from that that 'if you didn't bloody well like it you'll bloody well have to lump it, won't you!'

I decided then and there I wouldn't like it and I'd lump it as little as I could so that at my commission interview I was obliged regretfully to announce that for all of five years in an OTC I had not even attempted 'B' certificate and had remained a private from first till last.

But here at last, on *Indomitable*, a dividend was being paid to obstinacy — instead of sharing some sweltering cabin on the starboard side, I was cool and fresh in my cubby hole, afloat it seemed in the air itself, with salt in my nostrils instead of oil and the light by which my thoughts were lit, the phosphorescence and the stars.

These were the nights. The days were pleasant too. I played a lot of bridge and poker but mostly the days were spent on deck, pacing with others, disbelievingly, the flight deck, refusing mentally to accept it was possible to unstick in so ridiculously short a length. There were a few odd incidents but not too many — just one of note. *Indomitable* carried its own Hurricanes for defence which were catapulted off. Under their bellies were great hooks which when the pilot landed caught in the arrester wire, it being accepted that it was impossible to land and stop a Hurricane in the length of the flight deck otherwise. There was a man called 'Bats' who held in his hands two indicators like table tennis bats with long handles, not unlike those for directing passenger aircraft into their terminal bays on landing, and one of his tasks was to wave a pilot to go round again if he appeared to be over-shooting.

On this occasion Bats so instructed but the pilot either misreading the signal or preferring his own judgement continued his approach until by the time he decided perhaps he had better go round again he had left it fractionally too late and his hook caught in the arrester wire at the precise moment he opened up his throttle. And there, for fascinating moments, the matter rested doubtfully. The Hurricane stayed where it was, motionless, ten feet above the deck, pointing to the sky like some huge bird straining at a leash, its engine roaring and its propeller creating a tremendous gale. The wire on the other hand, taut as a V-shaped iron bar, resisted. It was clear neither would give way and the expression on the poor pilot's face was a study in consternation. In the end it was propeller torque which settled things slowly turning the Hurricane to the port side of the ship to deposit it as the pilot throttled back and the hook was slipped in the most undignified of positions athwart a gun turret.

But best of all were the many hours we spent sitting on the very front edge of the *Indomitable*. This was cambered in the most restful and convenient manner and there was a little fence which provided a footrest all the way along. One was suspended over the sea and could feel the prow cut the glorious blue of the Indian Ocean and watch the flying fish leap and scatter and fly like Spitfires by the hour. And again we would comment as we had in Khartoum that really it was the most wonderful of wars and the important thing to see it never ended.

★ ★ ★

On January 27th having seen no land apart from the incomparably beautiful green and white foaming surf and the yellow green palm studded horseshoe of the Chagos Archipelago the two squadrons were summoned to a flight deck briefing delivered by the ship's commander.

It had of course been accepted by now that it was the Japanese we were booked to fight and here, on a blackboard erected on an easel, the commander chalked their advances so far as known. In Malaya the enemy were as far south as Mersing, about one hundred miles from Singapore itself and as it so happened on that very day — and who knows but perhaps at that very hour — General Percival made the decision to fall back to the island. Meanwhile in Burma, invaded from Siam, Moulmein had fallen; in Sarawak, Kuching had gone and Miri in Brunei. In Borneo there had been landings at Balikpapan and only a day or two before near Kendari in the Celebes. The Americans in the Phillipines were being severely pressed after landings at at least six places in Luzon and Mindanao and the great glittering prizes of Sumatra with its oil and Java with its food and sixty million people lay naked, unprotected.

I suppose it would have been proper for the forty-eight young men ranged in a semi-circle, in their khaki shirts and shorts with their detachable brevets pinned over their left breasts and their motley peaked or forage caps or pith helmets on their heads, to have been, if not alarmed, at least sobered by these revelations. But they were not. The sun was hot, the sea was sparkling blue, the breeze soft and steady — and there was excitement and adventure in the air. The map drawn on the blackboard meant nothing to most of them and they had heard of few of the places spoken of before. They didn't know with any sense of certainty quite where in the world they were, their geography being in most cases abysmal. As for the Japanese with their feeble wooden biplanes, they seemed as the scent of a drag hunt or a drogue in firing practice. It was almost as if someone had arranged their presence as an excuse for this splendid jamboree.

But the Commander's voice was grave and he spoke stirringly of the deeds of derring-do they would no doubt soon perform, assured them he was sure the world would hear of them and wished them luck. They listened with due politeness, a trifle embarrassed by these eulogies and having in spite of all his efforts conceived no real grip on the proposition broke away with some relief to have a drink or two and talk it over.

What was curious was that no one thought to ask if anyone had any idea of the performance and equipment of the Japanese Air Force and no one thought to volunteer to us such information. Perhaps no one knew. At all events it never crossed our minds that in any field the machines we should have to fight could be superior to our Hurricanes. After all before the war the word 'Japanese' was almost an adjective for rubbish.

★ ★ ★

At dawn on January 28th, the first sixteen Hurricanes were raised by the lift and packed herringbone fashion at the stern of the *Indomitable* and by the time the day had broken bright and clear and the sea had lost its greyness we had run up our engines, checked our instruments, made sure our kitbags were secure in the bellies of the fuselage and had stowed away the few odd pieces such as razors and revolvers in side pockets and camera gun mountings.

There was nothing left to do but wait. We climbed down from the cockpits, paced the now shortened deck still disbelieving, checked and rechecked our maps trying to grasp locations, harried the meteorological officer, chatted and smoked — and tried to ignore our beating hearts. It was not until midday that we were ordered back into the cockpits and even then there was a long tense wait for the arrival of the escorting Blenheims; for an hour perhaps we sat, helmets on gunsights or hung loose around our necks. We were so far as I can remember: Thomson, Healey, Glynn, McAlister, Campbell, Kleckner, Lambert, Sharp, White, Keedwell, Scott, McCulloch, Dobbyn, Macnamara, Nash and me. We were, I suppose, a little self important, rather proud, not ashamed to feel sentimental about a rather unique companionship we shared. We certainly felt apart from other men once we were as now sitting in our cockpits with the familiar smell of mingled dope and oil in our nostrils. Our lives, after all, were three dimensional.

The Blenheims came and Thomson was the first to go — Squadron Leader 'Jock' Thomson posted to 258 quite recently, in fact barely three months before, replacing Clouston DFC who had been a fierce dark man with a formidable personality, a name to conjure with in flying history and who was, although we were yet to learn this, already in Singapore commanding 488 New Zealand Squadron. Beyond the fact that he was a regular and reputed to be a first class pilot we knew little of Thomson really — a man with an intensely difficult task ahead, to take over from a legend at a time when his squadron was to be abruptly plunged into a muddle of inefficiency, crushed morale and ignorance.

Anyway off he went ambling, it seemed, along the flight deck and was gone steadily, smoothly upwards. Ken Glynn, Junior, was his Number Two. He taxied out and opened the throttle; down came the nose, up came the tailplane, along the pitiful length of flight deck roared the Hurricane and at the end, dropped out of sight and disappeared. It was very disconcerting.

Third off was 'A' Flight, Flight Commander to whom I was, as very frequently, flying Number Two — Flight Lieutenant 'Denny' Sharp, piratically good looking with a wicked eye, heavy brows, uneven teeth and a small moustache. I followed. Gingerly. There was a shade more room now that three aircraft had gone, that much longer of a runway but Bats caught my eye and grinned, signalling me forward remorselessly. It seemed very unreasonable — to waste those precious few yards which might make all the difference between what happened to me and what happened to poor old Junior, run over by an aircraft carrier. But Bats was implacable — right to the very mark I was directed.

Go!

I opened the throttle with the greatest care sliding my left hand very consciously along the box, keeping the brakes on for the last fleeting fraction of a second, then letting them go as I thrust the throttle fully forward. I remember the moment with extraordinary clarity even after all these years, the sudden surge of power, the touch of rudder to check the slight swing to port, the exaggerated tightness of the cockpit straps, the closeness of my helmet all dangling wires and tubes. I saw the control tower hurtle past on my right hand and the sea of faces with the entire ship's complement except those on essential duty watching, felt a bump and a sickening downwards sink and saw with horror the sea rushing up to meet me.

Then the Hurricane was settling in the air as if it were a cushion against disaster and lifting me up and up and up. I raised the undercarriage lever, the green light went off obediently and by the time the red replaced it I was turning, anticlockwise and the huge *Indomitable* was only a tilted postage stamp a long way below. Ahead and above was Denny and higher still Thomson and, miraculously, Junior already tucked in neatly on his left. I closed in on Denny who grinned his wicked grin and stuck a thumb up. And looking down I could see like so many fluttering butterflies aircraft streaming upwards from the speck below, and the otherwise empty sea was not empty after all for there was Christmas Island.

We circled twice to form formation then fell in behind the Blenheim heading north for Java with the sun on our left high and burning hot. With the unaccustomed long range tanks the Hurricane felt sluggish and resentful yet still willing. It was an aircraft which engendered tremendous confidence, easy and even to fly, tough, with a fabric fuselage but powerful riveted wings; I could feel it objecting to the load of those tanks slung like bombs beneath the mainplanes much as a runner would object to a pack upon his back.

We flew in comparatively loose formation, rising and falling in the air currents glad to be sharing after all this time that curious intimacy of the air again. We had to keep radio silence so all we could do was grin and make small signs at each other and every now and then go through the exercise of counting we were still sixteen. There was no land anywhere and we were land birds, this vast expanse of cloudless sky and endless sea was faintly disturbing. The sun blazed on us and as our bodies grew stiff and cramped so the left side of our faces was burned red and sore, something not considered, and meanwhile our petrol gauges showed us using fuel at a rate which made the Malta to Alexandra project already thought suspect, look just damn silly.

After two and a half hours flying when I was just beginning to wonder, we saw the faint blur of Java. We lost height steadily so that by the time we crossed the coast we were low enough to fly over the vivid red and emerald landscape lower than a ridge of hills on the starboard side before we roared over Djkarta, then Batavia, with its red roofs and parks, its fine buildings, its busy streets and its canal flowing leisurely through the very centre of the city.

We closed formation, beat up the civilian airport of Kemajoran with triumphant insolence, broke into pairs and landed without mishap.

There was a welcoming committee and a marvellous light meal set out on a long thin table. There were Malays to serve us, dressed in sarongs and tunics and wearing curious hats like washerwomen.

There was copious light dutch beer. Outside on the tarmac seen through the glass wall of the dining room were our sixteen Hurricanes, safe and sound and my very own, Number 212. And, for the first time in my life, I was, although I don't believe the expression had by then been invented, a VIP.

It continued through the evening. From the airport we were driven to the Wielriders Barracks (later dubbed the 'Bicycle Barracks' and to become a Japanese prisoner of war camp) where we bathed and changed, impatient to sample Java. The cars waited and then took us to a club called the 'Holland House' where an equal number of pretty girls had been imported to keep us company. There was a band and dancing, plenty to drink, but something missing. Something we had never felt lacking in England. It was lack of confidence. An air of fatalistic gloom possessed many of these pretty girls. Although we were not to know it when we landed, Java was already lost to the Japanese; there was no will to fight and not the least hope of victory. As one of the girls, Trinie Venema whom, curiously, I was to see again from the back of a truck when a prisoner of war heading for some work site . . . as Trinie said to me:

'We are glad to see you and your aeroplanes look good but you are so few and the Japanese so many and soon you will all be gone.'

★ ★ ★

In fairness to Trinie there were only sixteen of us landing that day and naturally I could hardly explain that thirty-two more were to arrive on the next. In the event only thirty-one arrived and it was generally assumed that one must have suffered mechanical trouble after taking off *Indomitable* and put down in the sea. We had had prior, and strict instructions, that as it was impossible to land a Hurricane on the deck of an aircraft carrier unless it was equipped with a hook for catching on the trip wire arrester gear; in the event of engine failure no attempt, repeat no attempt, must be made to land back on *Indomitable* but one was to ditch in the sea and hopefully, be picked up.

By an extraordinary coincidence I was to meet the First Lieutenant of *Indomitable* on my way back home after the war was over and to discover two things. Firstly that some rather harrowing bombing in the dockyard near Hiroshima where I was to spend getting on for three years had been carried out by aircraft off *Indomitable*; secondly that the vanished forty-eighth pilot had indeed had engine trouble, taken a look at the Indian Ocean and found it not at all to his liking and ignoring the instructions successfully landed wheels down on *Indomitable* — and after only about forty hours on Hurricanes.

★ ★ ★

It was early when we took off the following morning — only fifteen of us because one of the Hurricanes had some mechanical defect. We lost Java almost immediately on take off and flew low over the narrow Sunda Straits which are breathtakingly beautiful, studded with tiny islets of bewitching loveliness — the surf the same green and cream of the Chagos Archipelago and with brilliant palm groves inset in the golden sands. We flew low and we stayed low crossing the forbidding Sumatran Coast where there is no beach but the sea comes in under the mangroves which quickly merge with jungle and where the surf can be seen flickering through the trees. We flew all the way to Palembang barely above treetop height across a strange new land of plantations, swamps and muddy villages. We flew so low we could see wondering faces upturned towards us and steamy mist wreathing through the branches of the forest. We startled flocks of birds and wild game which ran away in terror. We saw our first villages on stilts in swamps and paddy fields. And everywhere animals and birds and brown men and women stopped what they had been doing to take note of us.

We felt like gods and it would be foolish to pretend otherwise. We were gods as we flew in our loose formation fifty feet above the branches of the highest trees. Our bodies were in their prime — eyes, ears, hearts, lungs, blood all tested and found perfect. And to this superbness of our health and youth was added the zest of power, the thrill of danger, the taste of luxury, the awareness of uniqueness and the blessed boon of rare companionship. We were not fifteen, but a fifteen, an entity of individuals who saw themselves as only individuals to each other but otherwise an élite brotherhood — fifteen men in fifteen Hurricanes roaring across primeval forest sharing a common mood.

After two and a quarter hours' flying we landed at what was then and was to remain right to the end a secret jungle airfield, a vast clearing of irregular shape in otherwise all but unbroken jungle. This we were to call P2 to distinguish it from the civilian airport forty or fifty miles to the north east serving the oil town of Palembang and which we were to call P1. P2 had little to offer but its secrecy, quite without buildings and with few facilities, but was to prove of vital importance and to save many lives including my own; it was to be the cause of puzzlement to the Japanese who could not understand the brief continuing resistance from Hurricanes after P1 had been evacuated.

We landed not without mishap, two more aircraft being temporarily put out of commission through their wheels catching the deep ruts left by Flying Fortresses which had used the place. And everywhere the disorganisation of a hastily put together piecemeal resistance showed. When we landed the airfield was deserted, our Hurricanes with their long range tanks slung like bombs under the wings having been presumed a raiding force. The air raid sirens had sounded and with curt unanimity the waiting ground staff, their nerves tattered by the events of Singapore had taken to the jungle. And when they returned they brought with them the gloom we had sensed in the Holland House but shaken off.

But at least there was information even if it was of a somewhat depressing kind. It was here, at P2, within two and a half hours' flying time of Singapore, we learnt for the first time the capabilities of the Japanese fighter now called a Zero, but to us and the pilots of Singapore, a Navy 0. We were warned of a speed which matched our own, and difficult to believe, in fact hardly believed, a superior manoeuvreability. No one told us where the Navy 0 was inferior, which in many ways it was, because no one was in a mood to talk of cheerful things or even imagine there could be cheerful things to talk about. This was unfortunate. We were going to learn the hard way and in the process fritter away a golden opportunity. No one thought to tell us we had better fire power, a better ceiling and that a hurricane could take punishment which reduced a Navy 0 to shreds; no one imagined there was a tactic which in the end four of us would use time and time again against equally large numbers as those met with in Singapore with negligible personal risk. No — at P2 it was all about perfect formations battering the docks and airfields of Singapore and men being sent back by the Japanese their wrists screwed together by rusty nuts and bolts.

We were not dismayed when we took off again that afternoon, but we were perhaps chastened and certainly more thoughtful — after all it was quite on the cards we would run into superior numbers of these daunting aircraft before we'd even got rid of our long range tanks!

As we left, thirteen now, for Singapore we saw the second batch landing at P2. But not sixteen, eleven. All had reached Java from *Indomitable* but in landing at Kemajoran some had had brake trouble which was hardly surprising after the rough handling we'd had to give them taxying them along that unforgettable road, the crating and uncrating and probably lack of proper inspection. At all events one had overshot the runway and gone up on its nose and another whose pilot had been unable to stop had run into a third already landed and both were write-offs, while two more were unserviceable for other reasons. Thus thirty-two had become twenty-four — twenty-five per cent of strength lost and the ferrying operation not yet over.

North of Palembang the terrain becomes appalling flying country. The jungle is solid and without any exception whatsoever the only breaks in an endless sea of green are the brown swathes of rivers with glistening mudbanks with occasional thatched villages. Successful forced landing is all but impossible and an aircraft which crashes will almost certainly never be found again. The jungle swarms with wild animals, snakes, leeches and so on and disease of course is rife. For a pilot shot down or with engine failure the chances of survival ware negligible. On this aspect the 'History of 226 Group' available in the Public Records Office states:

Fighting and flying over Sumatra presented decided difficulties to pilots. The country was 90 per cent marsh or impenetrable jungle, and it was extremely difficult to make crash landings without writing off aircraft. The country was such that if a pilot came down anywhere but a very short distance from the aerodrome, he was lost unless picked up by natives, and the jungle was inhabited by numerous wild beasts including tigers.

There were practically no roads or tracks and the only possible method for searching for a lost pilot or aircraft was by means of Tiger Moths although even then it was rather like looking for a needle in a haystack. There were available a number of Tiger Moth aircraft belonging to personnel of the Malaya Volunteer Air Force who had come down from Singapore and valuable use was made of this force to carry out these searches.

It was a relief to strike the eastern coast of Sumatra after about forty minutes flying, to cross Sinkep Island and the Lingga Archipelago on the Equator and

Author's p.o.w. camp map of Singapore.

55

land in Singapore after two and a half hours flying without incident.

There were four airfields on Singapore: Sembawang, Seletar, Tengah and the civilian airport of Kallang. Of these Seletar where we landed covered the greatest area although the landing field itself was not all that large; but the remainder was vast with hangars, administration buildings, messes and in better times swimming pool, sailing club and so on.

We were guided in at dusk exactly eleven days before the Japanese were to invade across the Johore Baru Straits by a navigating Blenheim making an initial aircraft circuit while firing the colours of the day and flashing its recognition signals and there was time to see that the landing field was pock marked with minor craters. All landed without mishap but immediately, before most of us were out of our machines, there was an air raid warning and a great deal of noise and searchlight raking of the sky. But if there was bombing at all it wasn't at Seletar.

In fact I don't recall any night bombing

of Singapore, nor for that matter any bombing in the afternoon.

The effect of Japanese air attacks was far more psychological than physical and the chances of being killed in them frankly remote. There were six main targets for attack: the four airfields, the naval dockyards and the town, occasionally. The bombers came in groups of twenty seven flying in perfect formation and were escorted by a large number of Navy 0s at a higher altitude. The bombs carried varied from five hundred pounders down to small forty pound anti-personnel bombs and were dropped from the entire formation simultaneously. Thus there was one long hiss followed by a brief continuous thudding and all was over and the resultant damage almost invariably slight and casualties, if any, very few. I realise that this is not how it has been put about but it was how it was; the bomb weight dropped was small, the point to be attacked obvious well in advance and the soil such as to absorb much of the effect of explosions in any case.

One very curious factor in the whole

business was that at least while we were there there was never enemy air activity in the afternoon. There was one morning raid, or sometimes two, and then all was over for the day. It was thus possible to carry on with normal servicing of aircraft in the afternoon without the least interruption and indeed as the morning raids never took place until about ten o'clock there were several useful hours available from dawn until mid morning also. In fact, rather belatedly it was discovered that aircraft damage on the ground could be kept quite minimal by the simple expedient of driving fighters not actually in use into the camouflage of the rubber and then driving them out again when the Japanese had retired for lunch. I spent more time driving Hurricanes along the metalled roads of Singapore while someone held the traffic up than flying them in the air against the Japanese.

A vast amount has been written about the reasons for the fall of Singapore, but there was only one real reason and that was that the morale was bust. The bombing certainly had nothing to do with it. The fifty-four bombers maximum the Japanese used daily probably carried the same sort of bomb load as half a dozen American B29s which carried out saturation bombing of every Pacific Island before a landing was attempted. Aircraft hidden in the rubber were never damaged and even on airfields with the style of bombing used the majority protected by sandbag pens were pretty safe. As for bomb craters on fields or in runways these can be filled in with astonishing speed. Anti-personnel bombs don't represent much of a risk to people in slit trenches. What at any rate we used to do when not flying was to stand on the airfield watching the bombers approach and if from their direction we seemed the possible target make our way to the edge of a slit trench which we got into without haste when the bombers got close; in fact I should say there was even the time to wait until one heard the whistle of the descending bombs before one got in, although frankly I never left it quite that late.

The trenches were about four feet deep and very narrow. If you lay on your back in the bottom of one, which was my invariable practice, apart from getting muddy if there'd been rain you couldn't come to much harm unless you were so extraordinarily unfortunate as to have one of the bigger bombs land close enough to throw the sides in. This is obvious when one thinks about it. A forty pound bomb explodes throwing out its bits of shrapnel and there just is no way these can get to the bottom of a trench fifteen inches wide and four feet deep — they must bury themselves into the soft sides above you. Well anyway, it was how we calculated it.

The trouble with this sort of comment is of course that one is running straight into a herd of sacred cows which not only are the very devil to shift but make you unpopular when you try to do so. Still there's not much point in trying to write factually about personal experiences if one departs from the facts the moment they look inconvenient.

Singapore, Sumatra and Java fell not because of any vast preponderance of men and arms by the Japanese but because the men who should and could have fought them off lost their courage, were bust in morale or were cowards . . . these are different ways of putting the same thing, or rather nearly the same thing, for there is a difference between being a coward, being bust in morale or losing one's courage even if, unfortunately, when it comes to defeating a cock-a-hoop enemy the effect is the same — you don't defeat him, he defeats you.

It is human nature, and it is certainly good wartime politics, to put forward convincing excuses to hide shameful and quite unnecessary defeats. The guns of Singapore pointed in the wrong direction, the water supplies were cut off and the bombing was unendurable. In my personal view it would not have made the slightest difference if all the much vaunted guns of Singapore had pointed in the right direction; the Japanese did not cross the Johore Baru Straits in battleships, they crossed in sampans and rowboats and the like; the big guns' shells would either have whistled harmlessly over their heads and thumped into soggy jungle or knocked a handful off here and there. The water was not located on the northern edge of Singapore, it was in the middle; if an enemy could get so far as to cross with a numerically inferior force a mile of water and then take half an island nothing was going to stop it taking the other half; and if Pip Healey could amble out from a Sergeant's Mess with a glass of beer in his hand, eye with interest an approaching bombing formation, quietly put his glass on the slit trench edge, duck down while the bombs got it all quickly over with and then finish off a beer not even beginning to get flat in the absolute certainty there was nothing more to worry about that day, it was clearly rather removed from Armageddon.

The first territory taken by the Japanese and then recovered was Attu Island in the Aleutians. It was invested by two thousand men without, when the Americans set about recapturing it, naval or air support. After bombardment of a scale which would have made that of Singapore look pitiful, Attu was attacked by twenty thousand superbly equipped Americans and after three weeks retaken — not one Japanese was found alive.

Singapore was garrisoned by a force of approximately seventy thousand men and attacked by a Japanese force which had rushed helter skelter down through Malaya quite astonished at the speed of its progress and was less in number and only averagely equipped; it held out five days. About seventy thousand were taken prisoner.

These are facts. Churchill wrote:

Prime Minister to General Wavell

10 Feb 42

I think you ought to realise the way we view the situation in Singapore. It was reported to the Cabinet by the C.I.G.S. that Percival has over 100,000 men, of whom 33,000 are British and 17,000 Australian. It is doubtful whether the Japanese have as many in the whole Malay peninsula, namely, five divisions forward and a sixth coming up. In these circumstances the defenders must greatly outnumber Japanese forces who have crossed the straits, and in a well-contested battle should destroy them.

Wavell replied:

General Wavell to Prime Minister
11 Feb 42

Battle for Singapore is not going well. Japanese, with usual infiltration tactics, are getting on much more rapidly than they should in west of island . . . Morale of some troops is not good, and none as high as I should like to see . . . Everything possible is being done to produce a more offensive spirit and optimistic outlook, but I cannot pretend that these efforts have been entirely successful up to date . . . I do not think that Percival has the number of troops at his disposal that you mention. I do not think that he has more than 60 to 70 thousands at the most. He should however have quite enough to deal with enemy who have landed if the troops can be made to act with sufficient vigour and determination.

Well, of course, when we landed on that evening of January 29th on Seletar aerodrome we knew nothing of any of this but within ten minutes of ordering a drink in the mess we realised that the pall of defeatism was so thick you could have cut it with a knife. It was Java again only maybe worse. A horrible evening.

The next morning was little better.

I strolled out in the still fresh cool of early day with Bruce McAlister, the gentlest, the best liked, the quietest of the New Zealanders, a man of screwed up eyes, small in stature, undemanding. We crossed the airfield to our Hurricanes, protected by their sandbagged bays, close to the rubber, as it was called, which grew up to Seletar's boundary.

The ground crews were busy and working under difficulties. They had never worked on Hurricanes before, their spanners didn't fit and the removal of the long range tanks was proving to be a stubborn mystery. They possessed no spares and they had no supplies of Glycol which was the coolant fluid for the Rolls Royce Merlin engines. Above all the guns, the twelve .303 Brownings, six in either wing, were presenting them with an unconsidered problem. Presumably to protect them from salt at sea they were thickly caked with sticky grease of which incidentally we knew nothing — had we met Japanese, or even tried trial bursts we would probably have blown the wings off! Or so they said.

Anyway there was nothing to do but strip them down to each tiny part and clean these in hot thin oil and reassemble . . . and there were a lot of parts and a lot of guns.

We hung around, Bruce and me — not because there was anything we could do but because there was not much else to do anyway and I suppose we felt that hanging around was the right thing to do. We chatted, smoked, remembered the odd bits and pieces, including our revolvers stowed away in the cine gun camera mountings and retrieved them.

At about half past nine the attention of the ground crews began to wander and their eyes to turn with growing frequency to the sky. Not that there was any sound of aircraft — there was only the sound of birds and of the gentle shift of the morning breeze in the nearby rubber trees. The sun had begun to gather heat, the damp ground begun to shimmer

— voices drifted, insects hummed. And the war seemed very far away.

And then, quite suddenly, one man called something to his mates and the man working on my guns dropped the sear pin or whatever it was he happened to be wiping at the time back into the bath of amber oil and set off with the rest with one accord towards the rubber.

I never knew till then that Bruce McAlister could be angry.

'What the hell', he shouted, in his twangy, nasal voice, 'do you think you're doing? Where the hell do you think you're going?'

They stopped, momentarily, and one man pointed to the sky. I looked up and there in an otherwise unmarked blue sky was drawn a white circle, a vapour trail which even as I looked at it was thickening lazily and leaving behind the white sparkling diamond of the reconnaissance aircraft which had made it.

'So?' said Bruce, puzzled.

'Mean's it's us this morning, Sir.'

That made no sense — that circle must have encompassed about the whole of Singapore. So I asked him what he meant.

'It's what they do, sarge. They send a kite ahead and draw a circle where they're going to bomb. They'll be here in half an hour.'

And he set off towards the rubber with no more ado with the rest of them after a momentary hesitation straggling after him.

I was simply poleaxed. And Bruce McAlister was livid.

'Come back!' he shouted.

They paused, looked at each other, and came slowly back.

'Did you know,' Bruce said, with a cold kind of anger which afterwards when I recalled it I found astonishing, 'that there happens to be a war on?'

'Yes, Sir,' one grumbled.

'No sense in standing around getting bombed,' another muttered.

'Sir!' stormed Bruce.

'Sir.'

'You've just arrived, sarge, another dared to me, obviously considering me easier meat. 'You haven't had it like we have.'

I remember glancing at the sky and noticing that the ring was already broken, its remnants drifting off and the bright speck had either vanished or I couldn't pick it out any more. And I remember feeling then something I hadn't felt before for all the gloom of Trinie and the groundstaff at P2 — the prick of fear. And suddenly everything was quite different. For the first time I felt the presence of a race of whom I hadn't met one, the Japanese. Suddenly the rubber bordering the airfield wasn't just a perimeter but a screen and refuge. I was suddenly afraid. But more than being afraid, I was astonished. I had been afraid often enough before and in fact imagined that I was peculiarly vulnerable to fear and others, on the whole, apparently were not. Fear I had always regarded as a personal secret of which you were ashamed and which you covered up. But, I had always thought, fear, in war, was beside the point. It was something you had to live with, something that didn't control your actions. That was what war was all about. Or anyway one of its rules.

I looked back from the empty sky which suddenly seemed to hold the same sort of menace as does as a sea where there is reason to suspect enemy submarines to the small knot of bronzed and very nervous men with dirty hands and oil smudged faces. I was puzzled what, if anything, to do and so was Bruce McAlister, and this puzzlement was evidently read by the ground staff as acceptance of their point of view for to a man they turned again and headed for the rubber.

'Get your gun out,' I heard Bruce say and to my surprise I saw that he already had his revolver in his hand. I fumbled for my own with a feeling that the situation was extraordinarily unreal.

'Stop!' shouted Bruce to the back of the departing men.

They stopped, turning their heads.

'Come back,' he ordered them.

They came slowly back.

When they were near enough, Bruce said:

'Anyone who heads back that way again until I've said he can is going to be shot.'

There was a pause. I think we both felt the same as we stood there pointing our revolvers at that knot of unhappy men — uncomfortable and embarrassed. It looks very convincing when one sees on film or television this sort of thing taking place — when it happens it doesn't feel at all convincing: it feels melodramatic. And one feels personally ludicrous and gauche.

I know I made some sort of contribution but I can't remember what it was. I do remember what Bruce said and I remember exactly how he looked. He was in khaki shirt and shorts and wore, as we all did under our brevets, the squadron emblem, a small silver fern. His blue RAF peaked cap was at a jaunty angle. But the jauntiness stopped there. He was perplexed but determined, a gentle easy going youngster forcing himself to adopt a role which until a few minutes before would have been unimaginable and for which he felt totally unsuited.

'It may not be very pleasant,' he said, 'but there does happen to be a war on and we've got to be able to get these Hurricanes in the sky and you're going to stay and clean our guns until we say you can go and that's all there is to it. Now get on with it.'

We didn't have any more trouble and Seletar wasn't bombed that morning anyway. We became operational next morning, flying from Tengah airfield, and on the first scramble Bruce McAlister was shot down and killed. There is no suggestion intended that the men who failed in Singapore were a different breed of men from say those who stopped the Japanese at Imphal and then drove them back in Burma. Obviously they were not: they were a cross section of society no different from those in the fourteenth army. Change the two groups over and the results would have been the same. Morale is an elusive quality which depends above everything else on leadership and example and without which it is hardly different from a ship without engine or rudder which is blown by the winds of rumour and drifts in the currents of despair. I never felt in the short time I was in Singapore that there was any sense that there was a leader there or any coherent plan.

Apart from the rusty nuts and bolts through released captives' wrists which a lot of people talked about but none I met had ever actually seen and tales about civilians driving with their cars, loaded up with golf clubs, to the docks and leaving them available for anyone to take their pick and that sort of thing, there wasn't a great deal that went by way of conversation and such small hopes as were entertained were dependent on the faint expectation of vast, magically procured reinforcements which would do the job those already there had decided was beyond them. No doubt the easy going, high flying way of life of both civilians and servicemen alike in the months and years before the war had a good deal to do with the humiliations in Malaya and the Dutch East Indies and no doubt too the intermingling in an active theatre of war of mainly executive class civilians and servicemen was unhelpful. But whatever the causes the plain fact is that by the time we arrived in Singapore it was a doomed island. Had there been a Winston Churchill emerge in time it is just possible a change could have taken place and the whole of the world's history altered and perhaps it would not be unfitting to end this comment by quoting his own words to Wavell in his despatch of February 10th — although reading between the lines one senses he had abandoned hope.

The battle must be fought to the bitter end at all costs. The 18th Division has a chance to make its name in history. Commanders and senior officers should die with their troops. The honour of the British Empire and the British Army is at stake. I rely on you to show no mercy to weakness in any form. With the Russians fighting as they are and the Americans so stubborn in Luzon, the whole reputation of our country and our race is involved. It is expected that every unit will be brought into close contact with the enemy and fight it out.

4

Operational Against the Japanese

NO 258 SQUADRON made its first operational flight against the Japanese on January 31st from Tengah airfield having flown all serviceable Hurricanes earlier that morning the four or five miles from Seletar. These amounted to eight in number and encountered an enemy force certainly ten and quite possibly as many as twenty times in number against whom they had no previous combat experience. Two of the eight, those flown by McCulloch and McAlister were shot down but McCulloch managed to survive as was going to become a practice with him. Three other aircraft, those flown by Kleckner, Sharp and Nash were shot up but managed to make Sembawang. One Japanese bomber and a Navy 0 were shot down.

My Commanding Officer at No 56 Operational Training Unit at Sutton

Bridge in Norfolk where I first flew Hurricanes was Wing Commander H. G. Maguire (now Air Marshal Sir Harold Maguire KCB DSO CBE) who had, by coincidence, been posted out to the Dutch East Indies as Commander of flying of the proposed 266 Wing to be formed from 232, 242, 258 and 605 Squadrons. 'Micky' Maguire as he was known was a very personable man, experienced, intelligent, sound and tremendously respected by the pilots. Maguire had a plan. This was that the entire force should be withheld until all aircraft were operational, all pilots locally knowledgeable and a coherent tactical scheme had been formulated.

On February 25th Air Commodore Vincent (the late Air Vice Marshal Stanley Vincent CBE DFC AFC) Air Officer Commanding was to write from Batavia:

This afternoon we are actually down to 6 serviceable aircraft between the two Squadrons. All being well we shall get back to a total of 10 or 11 tomorrow. We are not likely ever to better that figure owing to daily casualties and the force is definitely wasting.

In fact Hurricanes in these sort of numbers had been flying from the military airfield of Tjillitan for about ten days and were to continue flying for about the same number. In other words because of the twin factors of combat experience and intelligent tactics a handful of Hurricanes was able to maintain at least a token resistance against hugely superior numbers for three weeks.

No 266 Wing would have comprised not ten Hurricanes but a hundred. Java was huge and had many and, importantly, widely separated airfields. The Japanese attacking it except off aircraft carriers would have had to travel very long distances, the nearest airfields being those of P1 and P2 In Sumatra. There were myriad islands in the Sunda Straits from which watchers could, and were to, give ample warning of approaching aircraft and there was a breathing space in which to arrange for proper radio communication between ground and aircraft and between listening posts so crucially to be found lacking in Sumatra. Far from being inexhaustible in numbers the Japanese air force was severely stretched with so many fields of operation to cover simultaneously. There is to my mind no doubt at all that had the Maguire plan been scrupulously followed through and a spirited defence of Java had taken place it is here the Japanese could have been halted.

Now it is easy after the event to make such pronouncements but the point is that Maguire made them basically before. But it was not to be. He was overridden and the Hurricanes were sent with indecent haste in penny numbers to the various places to be inevitably destroyed. During the entire time from arrival in Singapore on January 29th until we stopped flying just before the capitulation of Java on March 8th, the largest number of Hurricanes — of which I was one — flying operationally at one time was fourteen and I don't know of anyone who flew with more.

Moreover it was not merely a question of numbers but of experience; it is a salutary thought that when on April 5th the Japanese attacked Colombo Harbour and were attacked by fourteen Hurricanes, nine of the Hurricanes were shot down with five pilots killed and two injured, but the four original 258 Squadron pilots in the fourteen all escaped unscathed.

At all events, for better or for worse the initial decision was to send post haste every available Hurricane to Singapore, with the result that of the first sixteen which landed safely in the first batch at Kemajoran on January 28th only four were serviceable by the afternoon of January 31st — whereupon it was decided that all should be withdrawn to Palembang to form a new Fighter Group — No 226 under the command of Air Commodore S. P. Vincent DFC AFC.

This development drew a prompt and succinct comment from Winston Churchill in a memorandum dated February 2nd 1942.

I observe you have ordered the Hurricanes which had just reached Singapore to Palembang. Should be grateful for some explanation of this new decision, which appears at first sight to indicate despair of holding Singapore.

General Wavell answered on the following day:

Decision to withdraw majority fighters to Sumatra was taken during my visit to Singapore with Peirse on January 29th. Withdrawal of troops into Singapore exposes three out of four of island's aerodromes to artillery fire. Increased scale air attacks on aerodrome has already necessitated withdrawal bombers to more secure bases in Sumatra. Loss of Malaya emphasises vital importance of holding Southern Sumatra and maintenance there for offensive operations to reduce scale of attacks on Singapore. Fighter defence of the aerodromes essential.

To leave fighters on exposed aerodromes in Singapore would be to invite their destruction in a few days. Meanwhile every effort being made to maintain fighter defence by keeping equivalent of one squadron on

Kallang aerodrome, and by using other aerodromes as circumstances permit for refuelling fighters operating from Sumatra.

Consider these dispositions offer best prospect of air defence of Singapore, which there is every intention and hope of holding.

Churchill replied:

I am relieved to learn that you intend to maintain fighter defence of Singapore by refuelling Hurricanes operating from Sumatra.

2. Nevertheless it is a grievous disadvantage that the bulk of your fighter force should be unable to intercept from their base and should have to waste so much time flying between Sumatra and Singapore.

3. Although I realise the risks to which aeroplanes on Singapore would be exposed, I am not clear that the need for fighter defence at the Sumatra bases will be strongly felt so long as the Japanese are engaged with Singapore. Moreover we hope to send you about

ninety more Hurricanes by *Athene* and *Indomitable* before the end of February. I therefore hope that all proper risks will be taken in supporting Singapore with fighters.

Wavell's decision does not seem to have been properly thought through. It is practically not possible for a single squadron of short range fighters to continue to exist on a single airfield for any length of time against a superior air force which uses intelligent tactics. All that air force needs to do is to send batches of fighters at hourly intervals to circuit the home airfield and the home based fighters will either crash through being short of fuel or will be shot down like sitting ducks when with wheels and flaps down they come into land. The fact that this simple tactic never seemed to cross the Japanese mind in Singapore, in Sumatra or in Java is neither here nor there.

Again it was quite impossible for Hurricanes operating from Sumatra to serve any really practical purpose so far as Singapore was concerned. Without long range tanks Singapore was out of range; with long range tanks the fighting superiority of the Navy 0s would have been crucifying. In fact, as will be mentioned later, there was just one attempt to use Sumatra as a base for supporting offensive operations in Malaya and the result was disastrous — although admittedly for different reasons.

Finally it should be said that the general tone of this correspondence conveys the impression of there being far many more Hurricanes on Singapore than in fact there were. I was not one of those who withdrew to Palembang nor one of those who flew at Kallang because my aircraft was at Tengah and unserviceable. The place was a morgue, the messes empty, the billiard room deserted, the bar a silent place. Practically speaking Pip Healey and I had the place to ourselves and the only diversion was driving Hurricanes in and out of the rubber and watching the air raids.

Meanwhile, as Wavell had undertaken, Kallang airfield continued to be used operationally with a makeshift squadron out of pilots from 258, 232 and

488 Squadrons. 285's contribution was Kleckner, Donahue and Sharp — and Healey the moment his Hurricane was serviceable.

It was a very solitary feeling being the last pilot of a squadron on an empty airfield chivvying unwilling ground staff to put my aircraft right. On the evening of February 2nd the gloom was suddenly lifted when, totally unexpectedly, the balance of 258 Squadron returned to Tengah on a mission to escort Blenheims and Lockheed Hudsons of 225 Group on a drawn-up country raid on the enemy occupied airfield of Kluang. The strident roar of aircraft engines after the unnerving silence was a joy.

But it was to be short lived.

On the following morning we went out to our aircraft, my own serviceable at last, only to find them with their gun panels removed, the guns unarmed and no ground staff in sight. There had been, one gathered, contrary orders given although no one knew by whom. Nothing could be done in time. The Hudsons due to bomb at dawn were already on their way, the Blenheims, due to follow at first light and attack after ground strafing by their attendant Hurricanes, were already airborne. So the bombers went alone and the Japanese were waiting for them. It was disaster. The Hurricanes returned in shame to Palembang and I went with them.

We had a last look at doomed Singapore we had done nothing to assist. There were oil tanks ablaze and smoke was drifting lazily over the island which was defeated even before it was invaded. I remember raising my hand in a melodramatic gesture — but then it felt a melodramatic moment.

Meanwhile the squadron at Kallang continued to operate and not at all unsuccessfully and curiously as distinct from elsewhere the ground staff was by all accounts pugnacious. We were to find the same in Palembang and in Java but this was more understandable as new men who hadn't been subjected to the slow crumbling of morale in Malaya and Singapore had arrived from England. But the ground staff at Kallang with the Japanese already on the island and with the other airfields occupied or under shellfire found a sense of purpose which allowed flying to continue until February 10th when the last of 258 withdrew to Palembang — Donahue, Kleckner and Sharp. Healey had to be left behind because only pilots with an aeroplane could fly away — the rest had to take their chance. Only Donahue and Kleckner arrived at P1. Sharp had force landed on an island en route from which he managed to escape rejoining the squadron remnants in Burma while Pip Healey turned up again in Java after a harrowing much bombed voyage.

5

First Days in Palembang

THE squadron landed at P1 which was about ten miles north of the town of Palembang with its oil installations at nearby Pladjoe. It had been built as a civilian airport mainly for use by KLM and possessed two runways the main one being about 1,300 metres long and running north and south and the shorter one of about 800 metres length crossing this at a slightly oblique west to east angle so that from above the two made a somewhat boss eyed cross. The road from Palembang running northwards passed by the west side of the airfield and very near to it, in the south west corner and pretty much at the end of the main runway, was the airport terminal building, a, for those days, modern glass and concrete structure which we were to use as a dispersal building.

The airport had been created out of

thick wet jungle except that to the east the ground rose to a low more open ridge behind which lay thin scrub covering swampy ground. The north-east angle between the two runways was also thick jungle and swamp. Unfortunately it was not possible to disperse aircraft in the rubber as in Singapore owing to the wet nature of the ground and Hurricanes on readiness were parked both along the narrowish strip between main runway and road and in the equally narrow strip south of the smaller runway; additionally there was a dispersal area for unserviceable or damaged aircraft in a largish oval cut out of the jungle with access to the smaller runway and this was furnished with pens to protect parked aircraft from attack by air except of course on the access sides. These pens were pretty much standard wherever the RAF was operating and were tremendously effective in reducing the damage to aircraft in strafing or bombing attacks. When one sees film of the attack on Pearl Harbor, and the neat straight lines of meticulously parked aircraft all of which could be destroyed or damaged in a single attacking run one really does wonder at the thinking.

There were no hangars nor much in the way of buildings from which to operate the forces which for all practical purposes were to comprise the greater part of the defence of and effort from this vitally strategic and huge land mass of Sumatra, a country more than 1,100 miles in length and averaging about 200 in width — in other words half as long again as Italy and, except where Italy widens in the north, about half as wide again as well.

As Air Commodore Vincent (who I have been told was the only man to have shot down a German aircraft in both wars) was to write in compiling the *History of 226 Group* of the position on February 2nd:

'Accommodation at P1 Aerodrome was non-existent. There were no cooking facilities, dispersal huts, water, heavy A.A. and very few slit trenches and the defence consisted of a few Dutch Bofors guns and a handful of Dutch ground troops.

'There was complete lack of transport. The position improved slightly later but there were substantial deficiencies throughout operations in Sumatra (and Java). Not only was it extremely difficult to find sufficient transport for conveying ground personnel to the aerodrome, but there were no vehicles for use of defence personnel so that the sections were unable to move rapidly in the event of attack . . .

'The Dutch had a small operations room in Palembang with a single and bad telephone line to the aerodrome connected with the duty pilot. No lines were available to dispersal points. The position was not and could not be remedied owing to lack of equipment. R/T to aircraft was most unsatisfactory. The transmitter was in the Navy building some considerable distance away and any transmissions had to be sent over the telephone to this building and then transmitted by someone else — in some cases a Dutchman — who was quite unaccustomed to this work. The receiver consisted of a small private wireless set in the operations room. This set was much influenced by the daily heavy electrical storms. The Ops table consisted merely of a 1:500,000 map with a small number of Observer Corps posts marked on it, and there were no means of plotting enemy or friendly aircraft or any other information.

'The Observer Corps consisted of a number of posts arranged in two concentric circles around Palembang, one at 50 kilometres radius and one at 100 kilometres radius. In addition there were a few posts considerably further out — one at the North end of Banka Island, one at the mouth of the Moesi River and one at Tanjong Pinang Island just south of Singapore. These last two were of great assistance, but the other posts were comparatively thinly manned, aircraft recognition was virtually non-existent and in general the warning was given from the 50 kilometre posts. This gave very little time (about five minutes) to sound the alarm and get the fighters in the air. Communication between the posts and centre was by W/T operated by locally trained natives or by means of tapping telephone wires . . .

'There was no RDF (Radio Direction Finding) and no D/F for homing aircraft and in bad weather this deficiency was a serious handicap particularly in view of the daily tropical storms which made flying extremely unpleasant and homing very difficult.

'There was no VHF, the aircraft being fitted with H/F sets which were in many cases unsatisfactory.

'Hurricane tool kits were almost non-existent and it was necessary to service aircraft with any tools which could be locally purchased or made. Aircraft spares were similarly almost nonexistent and supplies of ammunition particularly AP (Armour Piercing) and de Wilde were extremely low, as were glycol and oxygen supplies. There were no battery charging facilities at the aerodrome and no battery chargers for the aircraft. 258 Squadron Hurricane aircraft were serviced by Buffalo ground crews, and all these factors contributed to a low state of serviceability.

'The majority of pilots were straight from OTU's (Operational Training Units) and with the exception of the CO's and two or three Flight Commanders, all pilots were completely inexperienced operationally.'

The only point of difference I have with this admirable analysis so far as 258 was concerned is the comment on operational experience. The majority of its pilots were not straight from OTU's (although some were) and, for example, I personally had about 160 operational hours on Hurricanes and I would have said this was a good deal less than quite a number if not the majority of other pilots. Again it was not correct that apart from CO's and two or three flight commanders, all pilots were completely inexperienced operationally — the squadron apart from its normal duties of convoy patrols etc had spent much of the previous summer on daily fighter sweeps over France where it had seen some, although admittedly limited action. Moreover quite a few pilots, of which again I was one having been previously with No 3 Squadron, had been with other fighter squadrons before joining 258.

However, in general terms, the squadron was certainly rather green although I believe this could have been considerably discounted if the Maguire formula had been adopted when the squadron would

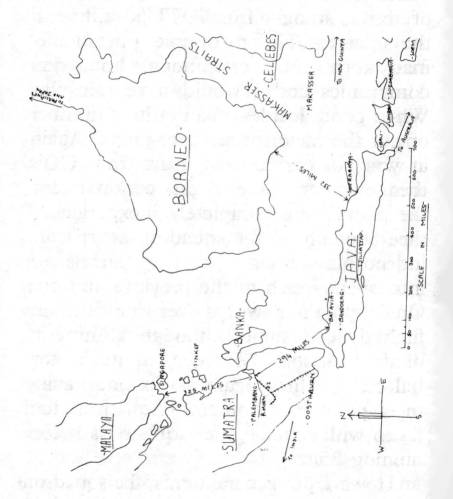

Map of theatre of operations drawn by Author in p.o.w. camp.

have given a far better account of itself than under the circumstances it was able to.

The Vincent analysis gives an indication of the extreme difficulties under which the squadron had to operate. Of all the many problems that relating to radio communication was the most serious. When one thinks of the Battle of Britain one visualises organised operational tables at which Waafs trained for their job under the control of experienced officers, plot the approach of enemy aircraft, giving the defending fighters reasonable if not indeed ample time to put themselves into an advantageous attacking position. One thinks of commanding officer or flight commander receiving a stream of information listened into by the balance of the formation on the basis of which he can make decisions and issue instructions. One thinks of one aircraft being able to warn another of an enemy on its tail, of a myriad of alternative fields at which a damaged aircraft or one short of petrol can land, of the homing instructions given to a wounded pilot or one who has lost his way or finds himself in cloud over hilly country.

There was nothing like this in Sumatra and it was to be only marginally better in Java. It was not merely that radio intercommunication was always bad, which it always was, but that sometimes it did not exist at all. One flew deaf and dumb over hundreds of miles of impenetrable and unbroken jungle where each mile looked identical to the rest and where the only way of getting back when lost was to fly until one found a river and hoping it was the Moesi, which it by no means always was, fly along it until one spotted Palembang. One could watch with horror a friend about to be attacked by a Navy 0 and be powerless to warn him. One could not inform that one had insufficient petrol to reach base or a faulty engine in the hope that one might be sufficiently pinpointed to make the chance of being found by a search party at least a flimsy one. As can be seen this grave want was to have the most extraordinary and disastrous of consequences.

Again through lack of a sufficiently

early warning system pilots were almost invariably at a disadvantage when the enemy was encountered (although this was not to be so in Java and as will be seen the result obtaining was quite different) and if one was not actually running out to one's Hurricane and taking off in the physical teeth of strafing Navy 0s as was frequently the case, one was still busy retracting wheels, climbing hell for leather or still getting one's breath back. The sky around the airfield would be scattered with Hurricanes acting force majeure quite independently under attack from Navy 0s whose pilots had gleefully watched them taking off and positioned themselves most advantageously to attack. And when one had to return because petrol or ammunition was used up one had suffered damage there was the simple choice: P1 or P2, the one possibly still under attack, the other perhaps too far.

On the ground conditions were sometimes strange to the point of comedy. A damaged aircraft would land and ground staff race out to it, not to assist the possibly wounded pilot from his cockpit, but to steal the oxygen cylinder from its belly to equip another waiting Hurricane whose fuming pilot couldn't take off without it. A good Hurricane would land and a wheel catching in wet sticky ground after a torrential downpour make the pilot's attempt to turn it accurately fail so that he chewed into another good Hurricane, making the pair of them at least unserviceable if not actual write-offs. A single Hurricane landing on the runway on its nose would effectively prevent any other aircraft taking off or landing until it had been shifted.

And so on.

★ ★ ★

From all the above it will be seen that the two Hurricane squadrons which were to operate from P1, with P2 available as standby airfield, were ill equipped, and unready to meet any immediate challenge in strength from the Japanese. This was unfortunate for Sumatra had the capacity to become a terrible thorn in the enemy's side. A glance at any physical map will show what dreadful country it is, far, far worse than for example Viet Nam.

Without any break the east coast of the southernmost seven hundred miles of Sumatra is swamp running in about seventy miles from the coast and when the swamp yields it yields to swampy jungle. All this writhes with wild animals, snakes, scorpions, insects, disease and pestilence. Huge forces of Japanese could have been swallowed up and the country would have done the fighting for the defenders.

The only possible ways, which were the ways the Japanese chose, of assaulting Sumatra and winning its vital oil supplies and the two airfields without which sustained air attacks on Java were impracticable were either to unload troops into invasion barges and sending them up the wide and often unprotected rivers or to drop paratroops. Command of the sea would enable them to do the one, command of the air the other.

It is now so screamingly obvious, and should at the time to those whose business is preparing against attack, have been so screamingly obvious that it is mind boggling that it never apparently occurred to anyone. There were, so far as I am aware, no river barriers, no strategically placed machine gun nests, no preparations whatsoever against the water borne attack and as Vincent has made clear no ordered plans for rushing seasoned troops to deal with paratroop attacks which would obviously be limited in scale.

In the event the Japanese did attack by river and by dropping paratroops and as it was suffered the most hideous casualties but had there been by then a substantial force of Hurricanes to straf them instead of a mere seven or eight and a ground defence of even modest substance that invasion would have been easily crushed. It is a salutary thought that another dozen or so Hurricanes would probably have done the trick.

What was needed was a pause and that there would be a pause had been assumed. It had been thought by Winston Churchill, and for that matter the pilots of 258 and 232, that the Japanese bent on the reduction of the biggest prize of all, Singapore, would spare little thought or material for Sumatra. There would be, it was believed, a space in which to bring the state of readiness up to a reasonable level, to practise tactics, to become familiar with the terrible terrain and the, at times, equally terrible weather and by collating all available information on performances of enemy aircraft and Japanese tactics, be ready for the onslaught.

These hopes were to be brutally swept aside.

★ ★ ★

The flight from Singapore on February 3rd had been made in the early morning and in the afternoon, as was the rule, it rained in torrents. Later the rain abated but for a while the sky remained almost entirely covered by heavy threatening cloud with only a small break to the north. We, the pilots, sat in a line on chairs on the verandah in front of the terminal building facing the end of the north south runway chatting and smoking. The readiness state, that is to say the list of pilots on duty to fly that afternoon, was chalked on the glass. I was not listed having been on readiness through the morning, there being insufficient serviceable aircraft for more than about every other pilot to be able to fly.

I suppose as we sat there watching the steam rising from the runways as they dried in the stifling, heavy heat we were thinking and talking about doomed Singapore from which we had just by the skin of our teeth escaped and the fortuitous fact that with all that was going on around we were still unharmed. I suppose too we were conscious that we represented the approximate total defence apart from a handful of native troops of an island of which we might well never have heard before but turned out to be large enough into which to drop the whole of Italy and leave plenty more all round. And I suppose we were talking about how it would be after a few days to get ourselves organised and when the expected reinforcements of Hurricanes still in Java had arrived.

Whatever it might have been at the time it was the last to which conversation switched when we heard the note of aircraft engines. There were sounds of satisfaction; some of those in their chairs stood and strolled out to the airfield, others inside the building came out on the verandah, others again, including me, decided it was too hot, too hot and too sticky and stayed where we were.

I remember being quite impressed that with miles of cloud above, the Hurricanes had found P1 and thinking how lucky it was there was that one break or they could never have landed and might have been very pushed to make it back to Java. And it was then that we saw the first of the Hurricanes break into view in the small blue gap to the north in the mass of sullen cloud like overlapping slates which otherwise roofed the sky. Only of course it wasn't a Hurricane but a Navy 0. We watched the first and then one by one the others, still tiny specks, lazily pouring through the gap diving on us in the traditional beat up. It was the expected thing on arriving at a new station, to beat it up. It told everyone you were arriving; it made everyone stop whatever they were doing to look at you; it brought people inside buildings outside or at least to the window; it drowned all conversation.

It was only when the fighters were

comparatively near we realised they had radial engines, that they weren't Hurricanes. It took only a moment to realise what they were, Navy 0s and by then it was too late. The air was filled with the whine of bullets and cannon shells and the roar of engines. The first Navy Nought pulled out of its dive and climbed away from its first attack not twenty feet above my head, the blood red circles on its wings mocking us. Behind me was the sound of shattering glass and yards to my left a man was screaming and clutching at his stomach. The second Navy 0 was already into its attack seeming to be aiming directly at me and not a hundred yards away its machine guns and cannon blazing. I dropped and as it pulled up ran.

P1 was filled with running men: pilots on readiness running to their aircraft, ground staff running out to help them in and start them up, others with no purpose in remaining running for the jungle.

I began to run and then I had to stop, if briefly, because a few yards away I saw something which to me seemed quite incredible. Red Campbell was standing calmly, revolver in hand, aiming at the next Navy 0. It was useless of course but not a gesture. One does read of men who have no fear but they are very rare. But Campbell was one of them.

There is something very different between being a helpless recipient of general bombing such as a city's inhabitants have to endure and being the specific target. While the danger in the latter is obviously much greater there is much more to occupy one's mind than simply crossing one's fingers, waiting and hoping for the best. And there was certainly a lot of drama in that first blooding of this particular kind of warfare.

There were one's friends taxying past at dangerous speeds and tearing down the runway to do battle; there were the strafing Navy 0s; the shriek of aircraft, the shattering of glass, the spatter of machine guns, the pop of cannon and now the slow cudumph, cudumph, cudumph of the Bofors guns. Then there was added the heartening chatter of Brownings. There were air battles to witness against the background of the heavy cloud, a Navy 0 hurtling earthwards in a screaming dive into the jungle, a Hurricane eluding a Japanese which had been sitting on its tail apparently pumping bullets into it, another hit and showing the thin white thread of leaking Glycol thicken, yet managing to land. And there was Campbell, nerveless, reloading his revolver.

★ ★ ★

When the fracas died down I went back to the verandah and picking up my chair which had fallen over saw there was a neat bullet hole through one of its chromium legs. I went into the terminal building and there was damage everywhere and the readiness situation chalked on the glass was in pieces on the floor. I tried to make a jigsaw to find out who was flying. The Bofors guns had fallen silent and the sky was clearing fast of clouds. I went out again and now there were no aircraft to be seen, only the more distant sound of them and men were fast emerging from the jungle.

Although I do not remember this myself there was an ironical result from the strafing which might have made the Japanese smile had they been aware of it. Apparently (I had this from Thomson), there was a splendid picture of a line of British battleships, white ensigns proudly flying, hung on a wall of the terminal building. By the time the Navy 0s had finished with us this impressive piece of propaganda was hanging at a drunken angle threatening to hit the floor at any instant. This would not have mattered all that much but for its caption: 'The downfall of the dictators is assured.'

★ ★ ★

Curiously the attack had been an almost total failure. Of the aircraft which managed to get airborne all landed safely — mostly at P2. A few ground staff personnel were killed and wounded.

None of the aircraft on the ground were damaged.

★ ★ ★

We were not always so fortunate and, in fact, one of the worst days of all was the next, February 4th, when the airfield was again attacked in a raid much better planned. This time there were bombers and the Japanese didn't make the error of having their whole force strafe in a combined attack. Again there was no warning and this time there were fighters waiting to pick off the Hurricanes taking off to do battle with them.

We flew several times that day and by the end of it nine 258 Squadron aircraft were missing or shot down and others damaged and in fact out of the entire force the only two Hurricanes which managed to get back to P1 undamaged were my own and Bertie Lambert's. Three 258 Squadron pilots were dead, one was dying, two were missing and three had been badly shot about and their pilots either baled out or crash landed in swamp or on airfield. The last were (Sergeant) Scott, Nichols and Nash; the missing were White and McCulloch; the dying was Keedwell; and the dead were (Pilot Officer) Scott, Kleckner and Glynn.

Roy Keedwell, with whom I and a couple of girls had spent the last night's leave in London had been injured, managed to land at P1 but in taxying in his Hurricane caught fire and because of his leg injuries he couldn't get out of the cockpit quickly enough; he died a week or so later.

Scott was one of those who had joined us somewhere between Debden and Port Sudan and I didn't know too much about him except that he had played rugger for Rosslyn Park. Cardell Kleckner was a huge, tall American from Florida, a wide eyed man with a splendid laugh and a tremendous personality, a man with the way about him and the temerity to stroll, hand outstretched out on to the tarmac when General Wavell en route by Liberator from Singapore to Australia landed at Palembang to refuel, and to keep the great man chatting in the blazing sun until the job was done.

'General', Kleckner had said wagging a finger at him while we gaped. 'May I have a word with you.'

And Wavell had let him have his word, or many words — all about why we were going to lose Singapore, what we should have done in Singapore and where we went wrong in Singapore. And Wavell had listened attentively and been heard to answer, and more than once. 'Thank you very much. That's a very good point, you've made.'

And when it was all over Kleckner had wound up, 'Well, Sir, nice to have met you' and by then the Liberator was refuelled and Wavell didn't even make it to the terminal building.

But by the evening of February 4th, Kleckner like Scott was dead, power diving, engine roaring, straight in.

And Glynn was dead as well. Ken Glynn whose father commanded a Naval ship but had to take a bucket with him on the bridge for the first few days. Ken Glynn — 'Junior', who strangely had at last broken his duck the previous evening. Ken Glynn, the much loved baby of the squadron.

★ ★ ★

That evening was macabre. It was our practice to meet in the restaurant of the Luxor Cinema in Palembang. We arrived in dribs and drabs. No one knew exactly who was flying that day or where everyone had been. Thomson had a piece of paper on which he wrote names as we arrived. When after a long gap no one else arrived we sat down gloomily to eat.

The experiences of White and McCulloch who returned a few days later brought a lighter note even if tinged with regret. The terrain south of Palembang was much more open than to the north and although bad flying country, did at least offer the chance of force landing in open swamp or occasional clearing. McCulloch managed to force land right way up in swamp and launched the dinghy all pilots had fixed under the parachute on which one sat in the Hurricane bucket seat, inflated it and paddled his way through the swamp until he came upon a canoe which he borrowed, leaving a ten guilder note pinned to a tree in payment. In due course he reached a village where the natives were more than friendly, regaled him with beer from a refrigerator which ran on paraffin and gave him the biggest double bed he had ever seen to sleep in in a hut decorated with old newspaper and magazine pictures. Rested, and recovered from the beer, he was able to make contact with Palembang and arrange his own transportation back.

Campbell-White had a more harrowing experience. He was chased, exactly as I was to be a few days later, all over Sumatra at treetop height by a Navy 0, struck a tree and ended upside down in a swamp. He was knocked out but fortunately the Hurricane did not catch fire. When he came to everything was dark and he assumed that he was dead; then, presumably on the Descartes *'cogito ergo sum'*[1] principle, he decided he must be alive and with much difficulty managed to get clear of the cockpit. After a time a tribe of jungle natives appeared and finding the scene a comical one, merely laughed at him. It was a difficult problem without a word of the language but by dint of sign language leavened with a few 'Wilhelmina friends' thrown

----

[1] "I think, therefore I am."

in he was finally able successfully to do business with them by swapping the petrol in his tanks in return for transportation back to Palembang.

He was, however, very badly shaken — so much so that he asked Thomson to be taken off flying as he didn't believe his nerves could stand any more of it. One would hardly have imagined a more unlikely suspect for psychological breakdown than Campbell-White. He had the most tremendous grin, the most engaging laugh and the happiest of dispositions. But it all ended well; he was to be flying again on the day the Japanese raided Colombo Harbour and to survive the war. I heard only recently that he is now a mining engineer in Johannesburg.

The days between February 3rd and 14th were hectic with the 14th to prove the most dramatic of them all. One was either flying and involved or not flying and watching the involvement of others. Much of the action was close to and within sight of the airfield and there was a great deal of incident on the ground what with strafing and bombing raids, searches in the jungle for shot down pilots and so on. It is difficult after this lapse of time to disentangle one day from another but certain things stand out very clearly in my mind.

I remember for example seeing in the distance a Blenheim quietly stooging along minding its own business and quite unaware apparently that P1 was under attack and I was put in mind of a childhood visit to the London Zoo's Aquarium. They were feeding the sticklebacks and what they did was to lower a piece of cod on a string into the tank. For a moment or two the sticklebacks seemed not to notice the cod dangling before their noses, then in a flash they were attacking it, burying their mouths deep into it and it was all but impossible to see the cod for sticklebacks.

It was just like this with the Blenheim — for a minute or two it seemed not to have been noticed by the Navy 0s and watching it, from the ground, there was nothing one could do to warn and nothing one could do but hope. But, just when it really did look as if the Blenheim might escape it was seen and suddenly it was like that piece of cod with a dozen or so Navy Noughts zooming and diving round it and then it was down, into the jungle.

I remember a bombed up Blenheim in the middle of the airfield on fire after one of the raids explode. I suppose it was about a hundred yards away, certainly not a great deal more and the sight of that explosion is fixed on my mind just as the quick exposure of a camera shutter fixes an image on a film. There was a huge ball of yellow flame, quite spherical, which engulfed the Blenheim at its centre and a thud of pressure against my chest — and the man standing beside me, near enough to touch, was struck in the stomach by a huge piece of shrapnel almost cutting him in half.

And I remember one incident which was to prove helpful in Java later. I had flown down with six or seven other pilots, ferried in a Lockheed Loadstar, to Kemajoran first to fly Hurricanes to the military airfield of Tjillitan and then to ferry them up to P1. This was on February 13th. There were eight of us led by Wing Commander Maguire. We orbited P1 twice, then broke up to land. Flying number two to Maguire, I was second down. As I was taxying in I saw that other Hurricanes were taxying out to take off and realising something was afoot, I took a good look round to find the sky suddenly alive with Navy 0s which had appeared as if from nowhere. I have always believed the coincidence was too great that the Japanese should have timed their attack as to catch reinforcements, short of petrol, wheels and flaps down coming in to land; obviously they had been forewarned by some fifth columnist of the eight Hurricanes setting off from Java and had prepared to jump them. But their timing was just less than perfect for seven of the eight Hurricanes were already down.

The only one they caught was (Sergeant) Scott. He was well into his final approach, at perhaps two hundred feet, already over the airfield perimeter and in fact about level with me still in my aircraft taxying in. I saw with horror a Navy Nought on his tail, slim, jungle green, with its disproportionate radial engine and

116

cannon shells thudding from its gun. I saw smoke begin to pour from Scotty's engine and I could even see his head as he hauled back on his stick to give himself height to bale out — and in fact he did succeed and jumping from the aircraft at eight or nine hundred feet landed by parachute safely near the airfield.

What was more remarkable was what happened to the Navy 0. Its speed in the attack could not have been very great, three or four hundred miles an hour perhaps, and even the recovery from the dive with more than a hundred and fifty feet of airspace in hand not remarkably severe; yet it was more than the airframe could stand. Both wings simply folded upwards like the wings of carrier borne aircraft which fold for stacking purpose and the Navy Nought crashed beside us in the jungle.

But perhaps above everything the incident which I remember best is that of Dicky Parr one of the 232 squadron pilots. He had been shot up and a bullet had jammed his throttle open and he made a most remarkably efficient job of landing, switching off his engine and landing very fast with wheels up — usually a much easier operation than might be imagined incidently as all that normally happens is that the radiator is torn off and the propeller shatters to small pieces and the Hurricane slides along on its belly until it stops. But that is at the recommended landing speed and Parr was probably travelling twice as fast. So in his case instead of sliding on its belly the Hurricane mounted on its nose and slid along on that, a most extraordinary and alarming sight.

Had it toppled that would probably have been the end of Parr. But it didn't, it went on sliding until it was conveniently far enough along the runway not to prevent taking off and landing and there it stopped. Bertie Lambert and I tore out in a Bedford. Parr had climbed out of his machine and was waiting, watching us arrive. When we did so he put his right hand into his shirt pocket and handed something to us.

'I guess I won't be needing that any more,' he said.

It was his left hand little finger taken

off by the explosive bullet which jammed his throttle open.

★ ★ ★

Insofar as this period is concerned the *History of 226 Group* while not entirely accurate is interesting:

'*6.2.42.* At about 11.00 hours the first attack was made on P1 aerodrome by bombers and fighters. The warning given by the Observer Corps arrived minutes only before the enemy aircraft, so that the Hurricanes were unable to gain height in time and were attacked in ones and twos immediately after taking off.

'There was still no reasonable R/T communication. Due to these factors and the inexperience of the pilots, four Hurricanes were lost and only one Navy 0 fighter, probably destroyed, with one or two possibly damaged. Subsequently three of the pilots — one injured — returned. (Author's note: This probably refers to McCulloch, White and Keedwell respectively)

'The advance party of the ground

reinforcements ex 266 Wing from Batavia arrived by air shortly before the raid with the information that the main party would be arriving by train in a few days and with particulars of the force that had just arrived from England.

'As a result of this information a signal was immediately despatched to Bandoeng that the Air Formation Signals should be sent to Sumatra to assist in providing more and better land lines, both between existing aerodromes and Headquarters, and also to the additional strips which were about to be commenced. There were no satellite facilities at Palembang.

'At the same time a request was made that the equipment which had arrived out from England should be despatched at the very earliest moment and that the loading of this equipment should be so arranged so that the most pressing deficiencies — R/T, W/T and aircraft tool kits — could be off loaded first at Oosthaven and sent up immediately.

'*7.2.42.* The Japanese again raided P1 with bombers and low flying fighters and a large number of aircraft was destroyed on the ground. Once again the warning came late and once again the inexperienced pilots found the Japanese more than their match. There was a number of bomber aircraft at P1 which Air Commodore Vincent had continually asked Air Commodore Hunter of 225 Group to remove, in view of the serious overcrowding of the aerodrome and lack of dispersal facilities. Air Commodore Hunter had undertaken to have all these aircraft removed by 0830 hours but they were still on P1 at the time of the attack and it was due to the congestion caused by their presence that the number of aircraft damaged or destroyed on the ground was so high.

'Six Blenheims and three Hurricanes were totally burnt out and approximately eleven more Hurricanes damaged together with one Buffalo and one Hudson which had just landed. In the air three Hurricanes were shot down — two pilots returning later. One probable Navy 0 was claimed with one or two damaged. In addition one Blenheim which was just coming in to land at the time of the raid was shot down and the pilot killed.

'In addition to the damage to the aircraft on the ground a small number of dumps of petrol tins were destroyed together with one petrol bowser, and superficial damage was done to the only building — Civil Airport Building — which was being used as rest rooms for pilots and crews.

'Immediately after the raid all personnel not otherwise engaged in servicing aircraft, proceeded to clear away the debris on the aerodrome in order that the Japanese should not ascertain from the subsequent reconnaissance the extent of the damage. Fortunately the runways were practically undamaged and they were in fact never out of action.

'One 3.7. and one Bofors battery had arrived. They were sited at P1 and P2, aerodromes and at the Oil Refineries at Pladjoe. These batteries were, however, without ammunition as this had not arrived from Singapore. The final siting of the guns was eight s.7s at P1, four at P2 and four at Pladjoe. The Bofors were sited six at P1 and four each at P2 and Pladjoe.

'8.2.42. P1 aerodrome was again raided (in accordance with the Japanese regular habit of three days in succession). On this occasion the Observer Corps gave a longer period of warning and our aircraft were able to climb to a sufficient height before the enemy aircraft arrived and interception was made as a result. The raid was of very short duration and little damage was done. No definite casualties were caused to either side in the air.

'The OAS, Air Marshal Sir Richard Peirse, visited Palembang and was informed of the urgent need for more aircraft and of the state of affairs with regard to the lack of AA and aircraft ammunition, the lack of spares and of equipment generally, and of the fact that there was virtually no ground defence personnel for the protection of the aerodrome. He promised to hasten the despatch of new Hurricanes being erected in Java.

'9.2.42. Work proceeded with the digging of slit trenches and the hastening of dispersal pens which had been commenced by the Dutch. Unserviceable aircraft were moved to the dispersal area and ammunition and petrol removed from them to lessen the risk of their being burnt out in the event of further air attacks.

'Group Headquarters Staff, together with ground personnel of 242, 258 and 605 Squadrons and Wing Signals (all of 266 Wing) arrived from Batavia and were all addressed by Air Commodore Vincent. The general bearing and morale of all these troops was excellent and raised very considerably that of the ground personnel who had come down from Malaya and Singapore. A number of these latter were failing to stand up to the bombing and aircraft were not being refuelled and rearmed during the raids.

'*11.2.42*. Air Vice Marshal Maltby, AOC West Group arrived from Singapore and was informed of the general position and lack of aircraft, experienced pilots and equipment. It was suggested to him that 605 Squadron should return to Batavia pending the arrival of fresh aircraft which were alleged to be on their way. But he decided that the squadron should remain at Palembang. The AVM stated that with great reluctance he felt it necessary to remove all fighter aircraft from Singapore and 232 Squadron was recalled. Seven aircraft returned.

'Surplus maintenance personnel besides continuing the digging of aerodrome defences were given some of the unserviceable aircraft to break down for spares and parties were sent into the jungle to attempt to salve all possible spares from those crashed aircraft which could be found.

'At this time the R/T was functioning comparatively satisfactorily between aircraft and the Operations Room.

'Wing Commander H. G. Maguire (Wing Commander Flying) arrived from Batavia together with seven Hurricanes which had been assembled by personnel ex 266 Wing left there for that purpose.

'*13.2.42.* P1 was again attacked by bombers and fighters but owing to the improved control by the Ops Room and the fact that the R/T was now working, and of the fact that sufficient warning was received from the Observer Corps satisfactory interception was made and only one enemy bomber got through. Three Navy 0 fighters and two Army 97 bombers were shot down for the loss of one Hurricane and pilot.

'During all these days aircraft were used for covering the evacuation through the Banka Straits but serviceability continued low due to lack of equipment and spares.

'Two sweeps were made on 13.2.42 to find and attack a number of enemy seaplanes which had been reported landing off the East Coast of Banka Island. No aircraft were, however seen.'

6

The Vital Thing — Experience

I WAS fortunate in that although attacked often enough by Japanese I managed to get through the whole business with only so far as I know one bullet hole in any machine I flew and my luckiest day of all was February 14th during which my own affairs were much affected by experiences during flying training.

After finishing Elementary Flying Training on Miles Magisters at Meir, near Stoke on Trent, I had been posted to No 8. SFTS at Montrose in Scotland to train on Miles Masters, more advanced, and much more suspect aircraft than the gentle 'Maggies'. I had done just over forty hours flying of which twenty were solo.

Montrose lies midway between Dundee and Aberdeen in the County of Forfar and the airfield is located to the north of the Montrose Basin and to the east of a narrowish strip of level land running between the sea and the Grampian Mountains. Weather conditions here are often bad and were particularly so in the bitter winter of 1940/41. Snow which fell in December stayed for months and for much of the time there was heavy cloud and mist; even on the cold, bright days there was the ever present risk of 'haar', that terrifying fog which can in moments bewilderingly appear and blot out a clear blue sky.

On a January day having passed my solo test and with a few hours solo to my credit I took off on some exercise or other and climbing through an obviously thin layer of cloud found myself in a sudden strange absorbing world which would have sent a painter's heart thudding. Below, the cloud through which I had just climbed lay as a level sheet out of which rose hills and islands of thicker cloud while above was another sheet of cloud. There were no colours beyond varying shades of grey.

It was a world such as I had never imagined, cool, tranquil and fascinating.

Between the two layers of cloud was a space of about a thousand feet which apart from the hills and caverns of more disturbed cloud seemed to stretch north and south as far as I could see. So for a long time I flew around enjoying the experience, exploring, making simple turns around the islets and the hills, skating along the sea of grey below or scraping the sea of grey above. Then, emboldened, I decided to investigate flying in cloud with the intention of returning quite soon to my comfortable world of grey. I climbed gingerly and for a while the grey seemed much the same and then it began to darken, becoming wet and very gloomy. Deciding it wasn't at all to my liking I began to descend as gingerly as I'd climbed, back into my open space. But I couldn't find it. I don't suppose the cloud had closed in so quickly, I imagine I had gone too far west or east. I began to feel frightened and became hamfisted toppling my gyro compass so that now apart from not knowing any way of finding my open space I didn't even know in which direction I was heading. In other areas this might not have been too important but here there was the danger of flying into the side of the Grampians whose peaks were certainly higher than I was.

So I decided the best thing was to climb as quickly as I could and to worry what happened next when at least I'd have the solace of knowing that I wasn't suddenly going to find a hillside ahead of me in the murk.

It was frankly a horrible and a quite extraordinarily lonely sensation with false instincts continually warning me I was about to hit a mountain this side or that or ahead of me. I kept my eyes glued on my instruments but found that with each passing moment I was more and more tempted to discredit them. It was all very well the artificial horizon assuring me I was on a steady, even, upwards path but every sense shrieked I was climbing too fast or not enough or not at all or turning. It was altogether a ghostly, unreal and unhappy business. But I fought the temptation to rely on instinct and persevered and by the time I had got to six thousand feet, I at least knew I wasn't going to hit anything.

But it didn't solve the problem. All around was the dark, gloomy, impenetrable grey and the rain making streaks across the windscreen and the mist streaming past the wings. To descend again was unthinkable. If I had known which was east I could have headed that way, out over the sea for perhaps half an hour and then descended with impunity. But I hadn't the least idea which way was east and I was quite sure, and I still think correctly, that to handle an aircraft in thick cloud and puzzle out a compass was beyond my powers.

So I reasoned there was only one thing I could do and that was to climb up above the cloud layer and set my gyro compass by the sun and above the cloud fly eastwards until I was quite sure the Grampians were well behind me.

So I went on climbing and for a long long time nothing happened except that I had continual moments of near panic when I found myself disbelieving the instruments more and more, over correcting, yawing, nearly stalling, becoming confused, imagining things in the murk, soaked in sweat. I became aware of the most extraordinarily strong sensation that the world had been taken away altogether and that all that was left was this endless greyness and just me in the Master tossing about in it.

But when I was getting pretty near the end of my tether the cloud suddenly began to lighten which proved the instruments were correct after all and gave me a lot of heart. I pulled myself together and went on climbing. Tantalisingly the cloud having lightened to this extent and indeed continuing to lighten refused to break while the rain had turned to sleet and then to snow and ice began to form upon the windscreen. It formed in a thin layer which was swept away by the slipstream only promptly to reform. This was followed by ice beginning to form on the wings, at first on their leading edges and then, not being swept away, thickening and spreading. By now I could see that I was nearly there for the clouds were yellow but on the other hand under the combined effect of the fall off in performance with height and the weight of the ice on the main-planes the Master was becoming sluggish. The altimeter told me I was at eleven thousand feet which seemed a fantastic height and was at least twice as high as I had ever flown before. I began to wonder what was the Master's ceiling even without ice on its wings and at what height you started to need oxygen.

At twelve thousand feet I finally broke cloud. It was a joyous feeling. As far as I could see below was that layer of cloud which all today's air travellers know and take for granted, above the bright blue sky and the warming sun.

I reset the gyro compass and headed east with only the nagging thought of how much range I had and the unpleasant awareness that I had to get down through all that lot again to bother me. Eventually, and very regretfully, I dipped into it and was soon recollecting ice and in consequence losing height much more quickly than I sensibly should. All the old bogeys returned and quite soon I was flying as hamfistedly as ever and toppling my gyro compass. Well at least it was a quicker journey down although hardly a happier one. I broke cloud at two hundred feet to find myself over the cold grey, wave flecked North Sea. All would now be well if only I knew which way to head. Of course it should not have been a problem; there was perfectly good compass in the cockpit. The trouble was that how to read it had gone clean out of my head, whether through the stress of the last hour or so or simply because I hadn't done my homework properly I can't now remember. All that ran through my head was something which sounded like 'put black on black (or was it 'red on red') and steer on the lubber line.' Or did you put the compass point on the lubber line? And what was the lubber line anyway?

I divided my attention between steering a course between the cold grey clouds and the cold grey sea and glaring at the magnetic compass. I fiddled with it, turned it this way and that and finally and without much confidence and relying far more on the fact that a north point pointed north and if anything else looked more like a north point than anything else that one did, steered what I hoped was west. And then there was nothing more to do but wait.

It seemed a very long time flying at a hundred feet above the vast dispassion of the sea. I came across a freighter plunging in the murk and wryly informed myself that it was a bloody silly way of travelling from one place to another when you couldn't stop and ask someone who knew, the way. But by then it was too late to change my mind and I decided to press on with the rider that if I saw another ship before I saw the coast I'd ditch.

But then I saw the coast, turned south rather than north hopefully, and as it happened correctly, and landed in time for tea.

What I learnt from that experience was never to stray far from home when the ground was hidden by cloud and one was out of radio communication. It was to stand me in good stead.

The other thing to stand me in good stead was experience in low flying learnt, illegally, at Montrose.

★ ★ ★

Item 19 in the 'Sequence of instructions for flying Master aircraft' is Instrument Flying'. No one liked flying Masters much and Instructors were not exceptional and anyway there is really nothing much more dull than sitting in the back of an aeroplane while some fathead of a pupil in the front with a hood like an Anderson air raid shelter pulled over him, yaws and bucks you. So it was decreed that when pupils were deemed sufficiently advanced the instructor's place could be taken by a second pupil who was entered in the log book as 'Instrument Flying Safety Pilot' . . . a misconceived idea in that it quite failed to take into account rivalries and conceits.

My safety pilot was a man like Campbell — he had red hair and nothing frightened him. If he had been at Palembang on February 4th he would have had his revolver out as well. He was certainly not the kind of man to endure sitting for an hour like a bus conductor in the back of a Master with me fiddling about under the hood. In consequence our mutual exercise of Item 19 was usually limited to a bare ten minutes after which we would head off to somewhere to indulge ourselves low flying.

There was between us an unspoken contest; whatever one did one day, the other bettered the next. You were, in effect, challenged to a duel; you needed more courage to refuse the duel than accept it. The records of Montrose, no doubt extant, carefully analysed would no doubt show the result. Of every course that winter about ten per cent were killed in flying accidents, the great majority of which fell under two headings: night flying, and incipient spins whilst low flying.

The Master was not a forgiving aircraft. With the dihedral appearance of a Stuka, its incipient spins were vicious and the margin between control and loss of control very fine. An aircraft is kept up in the sky because the weight of air below its surfaces is heavier than that above; the slipstream from its engines or the induced speed (as in jets) of its passage through the air, or where applicable a combination of both, creates airflows above and below the wings which can be designed to this effect. The maximum lift comes of course from the wings which is why the less powerful the engine the greater the wing surfaces must proportionately be; a rocket needs no wings. When aircraft turn the effect of these wing surfaces is diminished so that in a vertical turn their lifting capacity is nil.

On the other hand the rudder, whose previous function is that of steering an aircraft laterally, if applied so as to be sloping upwards gives, as the aircraft is turned on its side, increasing lift until when the aircraft is in a vertical posture this is at its maximum. With a rudder strong enough and a speed fast enough (or an engine powerful enough) theoretically an aircraft could maintain a vertical posture although of course in practice this does not happen. Nevertheless it is remarkable into how steep a turn an aircraft can be put and still maintain its flying position.

When, however, an aircraft loses its capacity to stay up in the sky it stalls; the nose comes up and then a spin follows. The stall is gentlest in a straight and level flying attitude, most vicious when the supporting surfaces have been reduced and the difference made good by an increase in speed and/or engine power. Even in level flight the Master spin was nasty, jerky and disliked; spins off steep turns were sudden and deadly. At the same time it would be unfair to suggest a pilot had no warning; there was a narrow margin between reasonable control and incipient spin (which was the definition given) which took the form of violent juddering which could be increased or decreased by use of the stick: pull the stick back the merest fraction and the juddering increased, push it forward and it lessened. Should the judgement be wrong and the stick be pulled back a shade too far (or the engine cut) the Master flicks straight into a spin which is not particularly serious if there is sufficient height to recover; under a few hundred feet, probably under a thousand feet, recovery is impossible in time. The aircraft crashes. Moreover it crashes in such an attitude that the result is almost certainly fatal.

Low flying as a sport is not a matter of hopping over hedges, something an absolute beginner can soon accomplish, but it is a matter of flying aircraft at, for example, a couple of trees whose distance apart is less than the aircraft's wingspan and then, at the last moment, slamming the machine over into a steep bank and thus passing between them. It is also a matter of doing steep turns in open spaces only feet above the ground. It is, particularly in a Master, both a wildly exciting and terrifying game. The wing tip points at the ground only feet below as if fixed to it and the world rushes round and round at an amazing speed while the aircraft is juddering fiercely; there is the certain knowledge that if the judgement is wrong, then all but instantaneous death is certain.

These were the games I played with Wilson and, I hasten to add, not because I wanted to play them but because I hadn't the courage to refuse. It was bad enough when one was in the driving seat; it was that much worse when one was merely passenger, watching the ground whirling below, feeling the 'G' in one's body, seeing the vibration in the stick it was almost beyond temptation not to grasp for oneself, watching forests approach at two hundred miles an hour with only the narrowest of gaps to whistle sideways through.

We got away with it but not everybody did. And there was a sequel. Early in January another trainee pilot whose name was Willis was detailed to do instrument flying with me. No doubt he knew all about the Kelly/Wilson exploits and no doubt he felt exactly the same towards me as I did to Wilson, if he didn't play the game then he was chicken.

So, and it was at his suggestion, we went off to the low flying area after we'd got bored with the instrument stuff.

'We'll just', said Willis, 'go off to the low flying area and do a beat up before we go back, shall we?' And he added, over casually: 'Just one.'

I wasn't in the least enthusiastic, having to put up with quite enough of this business with Wilson as it was; I considered it an altogether far more enjoyable business gently tooling round the sky than scattering sheep and taking the cobwebs off the trees and you were far more likely to get back for lunch.

But what can one do?

'Fine', says I. And off we go.

Willis performed the business with care. Having found an appropriate run which consisted of a series of stone walls parallel to each other and athwart our path he flew, straight, low and true, lifting the Master over every obstacle like a dignified steeplechaser. In the far, far distance was a wood. It occurred to me when I saw this that with any luck once Willis had lifted the Master over it he might consider honour had been done with no blood spilt and we could go home. It occurred to me shortly afterwards to wonder if Willis had seen the trees and if I ought to draw his attention to them. And then it occurred to me that there was no need to bother because it was too late in any case.

One moment all was blue, then green, then blue again.

'What shall we do? What shall we do?' I heard Willis shout through the tube which connected his mouth to my ears.

I honestly couldn't understand what the fuss was all about; by the skin of our teeth we had been through the top of a pine forest and were still apparently intact.

'Go back to lunch,' I suggested. 'We've done our hour in any case.'

'Look at the wings! Look at the wings!' Willis shouted back in an anguished voice.

I looked at the wings and nearly jumped out of the cockpit in shock. There were great rents in the fabric like those in a sheet which has been left to blow wildly in the wind and torn itself against barbed wire and from these rents long streamers of fabric trailed.

'Can't hold it! Can't hold it!' I heard Willis cry and glancing at the stick I saw to my astonishment that although we were flying straight and level my stick, interconnected with Willis's was hard over to the left. Hastily I grabbed it.

In such fashion with the holes in the starboard wing evidently larger than those in the port we flew along considering problems which increased with each passing moment. We had, for example, obviously knocked off the pitot head (which measures the air pressure and thus the speed) for the airspeed indicator was hanging limp; apparently we had a Glycol leak for the radio temperature was steadily rising; and we could only turn clockwise by raising the stick to the normal straight and level position and the airfield circuit was anti clockwise.

So we flew vaguely in the direction of Montrose hanging on to the stick together, discussing tactics. Willis was all for carrying on out to sea and baling out which seemed to me a poor suggestion offering the alternatives of either overdoing it and drowning or underdoing it in which case the damn thing would probably crash on land ānd for doing that sort of thing you were probably shot.

So there being no other imaginative suggestions and a dangerously high radiator temperature brooking no delay, to the utter bewilderment of the station we proceeded to make a circuit of Montrose airfield as contrary to the other trainers taking off and landing as a man travelling the wrong way on a Motorway. Aldis lamps were flashed and Very pistols fired and Masters passed by at close quarters in the opposite direction. Ignoring everything we shoved down the nose, landed at guesswork speed and far too fast, slammed on the brakes, ground looped one way, then the other, making a figure eight, then, petrified, shaking, clambered out.

Our flight commander was a man named Wooldridge. He came striding out from the dispersal hut — his long trench coat flapping against his legs, his peaked cap, softened by time and being kicked around the mess, low down on his head, looking a menacing figure. He looked at the Master, looked at us, then looked at the Master again. He went round to the front of it, considered it for a moment and then, reaching with his hand into the radiator, took out a fir cone.

We were lucky. They couldn't touch me because I wasn't captain of the aircraft and when they brought a court martial against Willis their case was weak because I, their principal witness, had gone down with pneumonia and been transported to the Angus seat of Cortachy Castle. Willis was fined a mere one

145

hundred pounds and restored to flying duties.

More than anything else these incidents prepared me for the stirring days of February 14th and 15th, 1942.

7

Invasion by Parachute and Barge

ON February 14th the combined squadron strength at P1 was fourteen serviceable Hurricanes which, as has been stated previously, was the maximum I ever knew achieved and it is interesting to dwell for a moment on Churchill's comment in the fourth volume of his *Second World War* that: ' . . . our air force at Palembang, mainly Australian squadrons, consisted of about sixty bombers and about fifty Hurricanes.'

The lack of reliable information getting out from these theatres of hostilities was perhaps only matched by the lack of reliable information getting in.

* * *

A Japanese convoy had been sighted in the Banka Straits, a stretch of water between the large island of Banka and the East coast of Sumatra. 258 Squadron was detailed to escort a force of Blenheims to attack it.

We waited, strapped in our aircraft, for the Blenheims to fly overhead presumably from P2 but they didn't come and the decision was made to take off anyway.

It was a splendid day apart from some banks of cumulus through which we flew in a V formation breaking cloud at about seven thousand feet having seen just as we entered cloud and partially obscured by thin cloud below the heartening sight of a large formation of Lockheed Hudsons heading in the direction of Palembang.

Morale was unquestionably high and there would have been a lot of cheerful chat going on which I didn't hear because, in company with others, one of whom was Bertie Lambert I either hadn't got a wireless set or the one I had wasn't functioning.

We got to Banka and we didn't sight the convoy, which seems odd now considering it was unquestionably there and in due course Thomson decided to return to P1. I had no idea what was going on and was rather surprised to find the formation turning southwards away from the airfield as we drew near it.

Looking about and upwards I discovered what I thought at first was the reason, a collection of Navy 0s above us and then as the formation continued serenely on its new direction I realised no one else had spotted them. The only thing I could do was to break formation, go to the head of it and waggle my wings at Thomson, which I did. To this day I can see him looking at me, switching on his transmitter switch, barking at me and gesticulating for me to get back into place. I pointed wildly upwards but the penny didn't apparently drop. Something had to be done even if I was the only one to do it; fortunately I wasn't. Bertie Lambert came as well.

The next ten minutes or so were filled with incident. There were not a large number of Navy 0s, four or five perhaps, which is probably the reason why they concentrated on us rather than attacking the main force now, on ground instruction, on its way to P2. At all events after a good deal of diving, climbing, and turning and all of us spraying the sky with bullets and cannon shells, I found myself with — as Campbell-White had a few days before — one of them firmly on my tail.

We were still at this stage a little thin on the ground as to the capabilities of the Navy Nought but one thing we had learnt was that it was more manoeuverable than a Hurricane and also at average heights at least a trifle faster. The question of shaking it off in the normal way did not arise. The only thing to do was get down low and quickly — after all, (I had the Scotty incident in mind), if I pulled out sharply if I was still there to pull out at all, the damn thing's wings might fall off.

So down I went using rudder more than aileron to skid weaving as ragged course as I could make it and one of the nine lives the war undoubtedly granted me was doled out then because by the time I pulled out at treetop level although the Navy 0 hadn't lost its wings and was still firmly on my tail, I, in turn was still intact.

From then on I felt very much as

I imagine a fox does when chased by hounds. There was no possible way of attacking the Navy 0; if I had tried to climb or turn to attempt to do so, I should have been shot down at once. The only hope was in ignominious flight. Of course it wasn't easy for the Japanese. One sees Bond films where single aircraft chase men round fields and finally machine gun them to death but to do that is nothing like as easy as it looks. The biggest difficulty lies in the fact that the body and wings of an aircraft impede the pilot's line of sight except in high wing monoplanes which a Navy 0 wasn't. If you're flying behind a man in another aircraft so long as he keeps going in the same direction it's pretty easy but when he turns you have to turn as well and you have to aim a little ahead of him or your bullets pass behind — and to aim a little ahead you have to steepen your turn whereupon he promptly vanishes from sight. You are now in danger of colliding with him. And if the chap is weaving in and out of trees you have to be very careful or you end up hitting one of *them*. Again even if you have the extra speed you can't climb up above him for several reasons; firstly you lose flying speed and he gets clear, secondly you lose sight of him, thirdly when you start diving down on him again (assuming you *haven't* lost him against the jungle) you've got the same problem of deflection — in other words you have to fire ahead of him so that he runs into your bullets and when you point the aircraft to fire ahead he disappears from view. And fourthly you have to be very careful when you pull out of your dive you don't hit the trees because after pulling out to the straight and level attitude your aircraft still goes on sinking downwards for quite a way. It really is much more difficult than you might imagine.

So I wasn't the only one with problems and I think I must have had the advantage of vastly superior experience in this sort of game. I make that assumption by reflecting on the attitude of Japanese aircrews I saw subsequently as a prisoner of war working on that same airfield of Kemajoran where we had landed three months earlier with such high hopes. When a bomber landed the crew got out and lined up on the tarmac waiting for the captain to dismount; he then called them to attention, they saluted, he returned the salute and dismissed them. In other words there was none of the casual relationship one found in RAF and presumably American Air Force crews. Equally I am certain the Japanese training schools would have been based on rigid discipline which would not have contemplated the possibility of the sort of high jinks of which Wilson and I were guilty. Nor do I think the Japanese mentality would tempt them to such excesses; they accepted discipline unquestioningly, they stuck slavishly to the rules. And I don't believe it is part of the training routine of any air force to have their trainees flying at trees less than a wingspan apart and turning to fly through them; it would be too wasteful on pilots and aircraft altogether.

Anyway, although occasionally I saw tracer making lines ahead of me and whenever I looked in my mirror I could see this chap somewhere behind, and although in fact he chased me over Palembang itself (as I was informed by others of the squadron not flying that day when we met later in Batavia) he didn't manage to hit me. I just hung on to the principle of flying flat out, skidding with my rudder and whenever I saw a couple of trees fairly close turning between them. Why, I thought, who knows, I might bring him down that way.

Well perhaps I did. I don't know. One moment he was there and the next I was using petrol and nervous energy to no purpose because he wasn't. In pieces in the jungle, short of petrol or just plain bored and homeward bound, he was gone.

I felt much better and reviewed the situation. I wasn't quite sure where I was and calculated I was probably nearer P2 than P1 and it was tempting to go there. But there was no good reason. I had no idea the rest of the squadron was already there, I had ample petrol still to make P1 and plenty of ammunition left. So I flew around until I spotted the town and made my way back to P1. I couldn't land at once because there were still one or two Navy 0s about, of which I managed to shoot down one, and finally I got in.

I landed on the runway and turning at the end where Parr's machine was still on its nose, although pushed a bit more to the side, taxied back to the south end of the airfield and brought my Hurricane round in front of the terminal building in its usual place facing the east west runway. I was rather surprised that no ground crew came running out to help me down, refuel the machine, recover the gun ports, reload the guns and check the oil and Glycol — I was also rather put out; I had after all quite a lot to shoot a line about. But there was no one. It was mysterious. I undid my straps, unclasped my parachute harness, hastily turned the gun button away from 'Fire' and put my helmet over it, stripped off my gauntlets, hauled myself out of the cockpit, felt for and found the step in the fuselage and jumped down to the ground.

And still there was no one.

I stood astonished, looking round the airfield. And there was no one. Nor was there any sound except the faint sound of an aircraft in the distance. I was never so mystified in my life.

All but two hours before I had taken

off from a busy airfield, now it was dead, deserted. All was apart from the lack of people exactly as I had left it — the unserviceable Hurricanes, the petrol bowsers, the starter batteries, the odd bits and pieces, all the paraphernalia of an active fighter base remained. Everything except the men who used it. The airport building glinted in the sun, the chairs the pilots had sat in were empty . . . it was for all the world like something from Beau Geste: the deserted fort with the tables laid but only silence.

I felt very alone, bewildered, standing there on this large aerodrome wondering what it meant.

I looked towards the only sound in that hot and empty place, the sound of another aircraft in the sky and saw to my relief it was another Hurricane coming in to land. I watched it land running away from me, up to Parr's machine, turn and taxi back. It drew up beside my own, the propeller slowed and stopped, the pilot doing all the things that I had done got out and joined me. It was Bertie Lambert.

We talked in whispers — two sergeant

pilots beside their Hurricanes on a deserted airfield.

'What d'you make of it?'

'Haven't a clue.'

'Where's the others?'

'P2, I suppose.'

'You didn't hear anything on your R/T?'

'U/S.'

'So was mine. That was you came up with me?'

'Yes.'

'Do any good?'

'Yes, I got one. You?'

'Yes. A Navy 0. And . . . '

A man came suddenly racing from the cover of the jungle shrouding the airfield's edge. 'Micky' Nash.

'What the hell are you doing landing here? Didn't you get the gen on your R/T?'

'Duff.' I wondered if there were unexploded bombs.

'So was mine,' said Bertie. 'What's up?'

'Paratroops! You can't walk out. You can't drive out. They're all round the place. Hundreds of the buggers. You must have passed their aeroplanes.'

One of us remembered the Lockheed Hudsons.

'But they were Lockheeds . . . I'm damn sure they were . . . You saw them. They were Lockheeds.'

'Yes. Definitely . . . '

And then the awfulness struck Bertie:

'Jesus Christ on a bicycle — we passed right over them.'

'But they had British markings . . . I'm sure they did.' I remembered the trailing flaps. 'They were Lockheeds. And they must have had British markings. We all saw them. You couldn't miss seeing them. There was a bit of cloud but you saw them through it.'

'You know what', said Bertie. 'The dirty buggers bought them from the Yanks. What a bloody sell! What a *beano* we could have had!'[1]

'You've got one now', said Micky, grimly. 'Listen!'

---

[1] In fact these aircraft were probably Kawasaki Ki-54s which have trailing flaps and much resemble Lockheed Hudsons.

We listened and from the cover of the jungle heard rifle fire. I forgot the Lockheeds.

'You're lucky,' Micky was saying enviously. 'You've got kites.'

'If they start,' said Bertie.

'And if I've got enough juice left. Mine's showing bugger all.'

'Me too.'

'Well you'd better make your minds up quick . . . '

Micky broke off. There was a thumping sound.

'Mortars,' said Bertie, solemnly.

'Hand grenades,' said Micky.

I wasn't disposed to argue it.

'What are you going to do . . . ' I said.

'Get the hell out of sight. Before they start shooting at us.'

I didn't like the look of the green perimeter but there was form to things.

'But . . . '

'If you aren't quick, you damn well won't start.'

Fair enough — thank you, Micky.

'Okay,' I said. 'Best of luck, Micky.'

'I'm going to need it. Best of luck.'

'Ta, ta!' said Bertie. 'I'm off. Best of luck, Micky.'

We got into our aircraft hastily, all thumbs reaching for parachute straps and shoving the ends in the quick release, scrabbling for webbing harness. I didn't bother with gloves but grabbed at my helmet and jammed it on my head with the loose ends dangling. Out of the corner of my eye I saw Bertie's propeller begin to turn and, taking a mental breath, pressed my own starter button which is only used without the assistance of cranking, or starter motor, in times of dire emergency. Only when the engine is warm and the oil running freely is it likely to be effective and if the engine doesn't catch quickly the batteries soon run down.

I watched the propeller slowly, jerkily, start to turn and then there was a cough and the engine roared to life. I thumbed up to Bertie whose engine had started too then looked over my shoulder to wave to Micky but he had already vanished. I opened the throttle and turned left along the secondary runway to where it met the runway. Normally I'd have gone to the extreme south end of the north south runway; now I didn't bother. If there was the petrol, I'd get off all right . . . if the paratroops didn't interfere.

I slewed the Hurricane viciously to starboard so that I was pointing up the runway. Even now I did my drill; I was by nature a careful pilot.

PRAFT.

P. Petrol . . . that's a laugh. R. Retractable undercarriage, lights red. Okay. A. Airscrew . . . fine pitch. Okay. F. Flaps. Lever up. Okay. T. Trim. Trim wheel neutral. Okay.

I took the most cursory of looks around the sky for waiting Japanese then slammed the throttle open. The Hurricane began to gather speed, the tail came up and the nose came down so that now I could see the runway stretching ahead of me with the mess of Dicky Parry's aircraft pushed off to one side and the jungle ahead. Halfway along, even less, I felt the Hurricane unstick and I turned at once to starboard raising the undercarriage. The red light went out and I felt the bump under my feet and the green light came on and already I was halfway round on my turn to P2 and looking down I could see odd parachutes here and there like handkerchiefs upon the trees. That was all. Just the parachutes and the green jungle of Sumatra which hid the paratroops and nineteen years old Micky Nash and God knows who else besides. At five hundred feet I levelled off; I'd have preferred being lower but couldn't afford to lose my way flying too low over broken trees. Forty, fifty miles to P2. I looked at my petrol gauge and it showed empty. I throttled back to just above stalling speed and crept along above the trees the aircraft wallowing uneasily. I didn't bother to look round for Japanese; had there been any I couldn't have done a thing about it.

Twenty minutes later I landed at P2 with Bertie following behind. When they checked my tank I had two gallons left and I suppose Bertie would have had much the same. We reported our claims but no one was all that interested and who could blame them. 'Ting' Macnamara had been shot down and all manner of others were missing: Micky Nash,

Maguire and others, caught on the ground at P1. And, as well, the news was through that the Japanese convoy off Banka Island had launched large numbers of self-propelled barges crammed with troops into the maze of rivers which were the delta of the Moesi River serving the town of Palembang in which were other 258 pilots who hadn't been on readiness; Campbell and Harry Dobbyn, Teddy Tremlett who'd joined us somewhere and was to be one of the five pilots killed on April 5th when the Japanese attacked Colombo Harbour. Others. All the pilots who hadn't been on readiness today.

And yet another lot of kit gone west; the new lot I'd bought in Java to replace the lot I'd left behind in Singapore. Not that that mattered. But one thing did. My log book. Left behind in that damned brothel they'd turned the women out of to provide billets for sergeants. Damn! That was a goner. That mattered.

★ ★ ★

Meanwhile in the jungle around P1 a small but fierce battle was going on.

163

Nash, who had been Duty Aerodrome Control Pilot for the day had been the one to report the paratroop drop to operations. A brief instruction had been issued which explained the sudden turning southwards of the balance of 258: 'Evitt and Tiger aircraft! Evitt and Tiger aircraft! Do not land at base! Land at alternative base!' This instruction given, operations ordered all personnel to join with local Indonesian troops, anti-aircraft and other units to resist the paratroops. But there could be no organisation amongst such a motley group whereas the Japanese were working to a prearranged plan with the knowledge that substantial reinforcements were already heading towards Palembang down the Moesi River.

When it was all over the tales from survivors were legion and often bloodcurdling.

Micky Nash trying to get through to Palembang with one or two others in a car was ambushed. The road ahead was blocked and as they slowed, realising what was about to happen, a hand grenade exploded at point blank range and Nash was badly injured. Somehow he managed to get out of the car and crawl, his mouth filled with blood, into a ditch. After a long wait some Japanese came out of the jungle and, crouching down, Nash and the others while unable to see them could hear them jabbering a few feet away. It seemed likely only to be moments before they were discovered; they kept deathly still and silent for all the blood in Nash's mouth and chest.

Then at the sound of another car approaching the Japanese withdrew into the jungle and one of the men with Nash signalled frantically to it and the two men in it brought it to a screeching halt and jumping out hid themselves in the same ditch about eighty yards nearer the airfield. The Japanese reappeared, looked in the ditch, found them and shot them — one and then the other, then came back to the first ambushed car, still jabbering. Several times they went away and then returned apparently finding this a convenient base. Discovery seemed so certain that Nash lay on his back in the ditch, mouth open, covered with his own blood, feigning death. Still they were not discovered in spite of one of the Japanese jumping the ditch to explore the jungle beyond it. After a while a third car came down the road. The Japanese held it up and the driver jumped out, pleading for his life; he was murdered out of hand. Still later more Japanese arrived in a captured armoured car and the ambushed vehicle being in their way they shoved it bodily to the side of the road where it hovered over the ditch with its wheels only inches from Nash's face but at least now hiding him.

It was two hours before there was the sound of heavy rifle fire and when this had died a column of soldiers and RAF personnel came in sight heading a convoy of all available lorries and cars making their way to Palembang whereupon the Japanese withdrew into the jungle allowing Nash and his companions to join the convoy which after continually fighting off rifle and machine gun fire and frequent ambushes with many casualties inflicted and received, finally fought through.

Nash was taken to the hospital where it was discovered that he had a piece of shrapnel lodged in his throat; after treatment he was taken south to Java. He could speak but his voice was barely audible and gave the impression of coming out through the visible hole in his throat. He was lucky to escape yet it was only to be a respite. After a tremendous amount of flying in Ceylon. and Burma, much of it in action, he was killed in a simple flying accident on December 19th 1943 in a collision while making a circuit of the airfield at Chittagong.

Another strange tale was that of the group of 605 Squadron ground staff ambushed in a lorry. Those not killed outright were ordered into a ditch and guarded by a single paratrooper who stood across the road from them juggling a hand grenade. There was talk of catching it when he threw it like a cricket ball and throwing it back at him which proved not to be necessary when, after an interminable time of anguish, an Indonesian suddenly strode out from the jungle firing from the hip. The Jap fell. The soldier fired again, advanced. At every pace the soldier fired long after it was purposeless.

But the strangest tale of all, surely, was that of Maguire. There are different accounts. The one I heard was that he stayed last of all with one other officer; they left P1 by car and were halted by a group commanded by a Japanese officer who spoke some English. Having informed Maguire he was his prisoner, he told him he must tell his men to surrender or they would all be killed. Maguire argued with disdain that far from being the prisoner of this pitiful little group, they would soon be his because he had two hundred fully armed men on the airfield. And at this juncture observing some of the paratroops advancing on both sides in a sort of pincer movement he told the Japanese officer to order them back which he did.

The parley continued and eventually Maguire, seeming to weaken, agreed to go back and discuss it with his men with the rider he very much doubted if this would have any effect.

'You must persuade them', said the Japanese. 'It is best for them or they will all be killed,' — whereupon Maguire told the Jap to wait for him where he was, got back into his car with the second officer and, turning, drove back and past the airfield for some fifty miles before they found another escape route.

An alternative account is contained in Air Commodore Vincent's *History of 226 Group* and may well be more accurate — but personally I prefer my own version.

Vincent wrote of February 14th:

'A large force of enemy aircraft appeared and after lightly bombing the aerodrome, paratroops were dropped at two places around the aerodrome and at Pladjoe about four miles down the river where the refinery was situated. The number of paratroops dropped at Pladjoe numbered approximately 300, those at P1 350.

'At this time all serviceable Hurricanes were away escorting the bombing force which had proceeded to attack the enemy transports in the Banka Straits off the mouth of the Moesi River . . . Immediately the raid occurred attempts were made to contact the fighters by R/T without success, owing to the distance involved. On the return of the aircraft later, the pilots were warned of the position and the majority landed at P2. Those landing at P1 were refuelled and rearmed and after unsuccessfully attempting to locate the paratroops in the jungle proceeded to P2.

'All available armed personnel were immediately rushed up to P1 to engage the paratroops. Owing to the shortage of small arms a large number of personnel on the aerodrome were unarmed, and during the course of the day the majority of these were successfully evacuated through the paratroops to Palembang.

'At approximately 10.30 hours instructions were received . . . to evacuate Palembang and steps were immediately taken for all personnel not actually engaged with the paratroops to proceed to P2. This order was cancelled later in the day and the troops returned.

'During the early part of the morning it had been possible — despite sniping — to get through to the aerodrome and some of the 3.7 and Bofors guns were successfully withdrawn although a number of casualties were suffered. The rearguard for this withdrawal was provided by RAF ground personnel.

'Although a number of paratroops had been killed, at midday the remainder had consolidated and were holding the road about three quarters of a mile south of the aerodrome and just north of a road block formed by overturned lorries which had been ambushed on their way through from the aerodrome. Unsuccessful attempts were made through the day to reach P1 with reinforcements, food and water. Repeated but unavailing requests were made to the Dutch to force their way through with armoured cars. At about 16.50 a company of native troops armed with mortars and machine guns arrived at the road block and commenced to advance along both sides of the road. They soon returned however and the Officer Commanding stated that it would be impossible to clear the road until daylight on the following morning.

'At P1 after the rearguard for the AA had been provided and the unarmed men got away, the personnel consisted of the RAF Defence Sections of Nos 242, 258 and 605 Squadrons under their defence officer, a handful of native troops, and Wing Commander Maguire, a total of approximately 70. The paratroops were engaged throughout the day and substantial casualties inflicted, but towards evening Wing Commander Maguire decided that an attempt should be made by the party to fight its way through to Palembang, as it was impossible to defend the aerodrome at night with the small number of troops available; ammunition was running short, the men were without food or water and it seemed unlikely that reinforcement would appear. All unserviceable aircraft and petrol were destroyed and the party started off but immediately encountered a large force of paratroops. Following a parley during which each side called on the other to surrender, the party withdrew and a decision was taken to escape to the north west.

'All troops were loaded on to two lorries and proceeded through the jungle towards the West and arrived at Benecolen after a week whence the party was evacuated by sea to Java.

'It subsequently transpired that Flying Officer Taute, Defence Officer of 258 Squadron was told by a Dutch Officer on 13th February that an attack by paratroops was expected on 14th February, and he was informed where the paratroops would probably land. This information was never passed by the Dutch to RAF Headquarters and the first intimation of its existence was received when Flying Officer Taute returned to Java with the remainder of the personnel who had been holding P1.

'During the course of the day it was reported that enemy transports were unloading into barges and small ships at the mouth of the Moesi River, and that the force was proceeding up river to Palembang. Bombers and fighters were dispatched throughout the day to attack this force.

'Towards evening on February 14th the Dutch Commander stated that the situation was well in hand and that all the paratroops at Pladjoe were rapidly being rounded up. This wishful statement later proved to be false.'

And of the 15th Vincent wrote:

'At first light a fresh attempt was made to reach P1 as it was not known that the personnel had left the previous night. The task was abandoned after it was found that the enemy were in full control of the road near the aerodrome, and after the party had been fired on.

'In the early hours of the 15th the Dutch Commander intimated that his troops could not hold Palembang — the large Japanese seaborne force was proceeding up the river fast — and orders were issued to evacuate all personnel forthwith to P2 aerodrome. This evacuation proceeded throughout the morning until midday when almost all personnel, including the wounded, had been taken across Palembang ferry, the only exit to the railhead and the Oosthaven Road.

'At that time information was received from the Dutch that the paratroops were advancing into the town and the small amount of transport which had not been ferried over the river was destroyed and the remaining personnel evacuated.

During the course of the morning all stocks of petrol and rubber and the utility installations were destroyed by the Dutch. Oil Refineries and storage tanks had been ignited during the night.

'All secret papers, documents and maps were destroyed in Palembang together with Ops Room equipment but the IFF sets were successfully brought to Java.

'A large additional force of parachutists was landed at P1 during the morning and these were quickly followed by troop carriers. Our bombers and fighters were used throughout the day to attack the river force which had reached within a mile or two of the town by midday.

'By means of what motor transport was available and trains, all personnel was transported to P2 a distance of approximately 50 miles, but by the early afternoon the position was such that it was apparent that P2 could not be held if attacked from the land, and orders were given for the evacuation of all personnel to Oosthaven, a ground defence force covering the retreat. Bomber aircraft were ordered to proceed after their last sortie direct to Bandoeng and the fighters to Batavia.

'There was still a serious shortage of transport and a number of Hudsons sent from Bandoeng assisted in evacuating ground personnel. In addition all available trains were utilised, remaining personnel proceeding by road, some transport being used for 'leapfrogging' those marching.

'Air Commodore Vincent proceeded through the night by road and arrived at Oosthaven early in the morning of the 16th to find petrol, rubber etc being destroyed by the Dutch and all troops being evacuated by sea. Lorries were sent back to pick up personnel marching down the road, and those whose transport had broken down en route. An attempt was made to procure a train for this purpose, but without success. Rear guards were provided by RAF ground personnel and all bridges were mined.

'All personnel arriving, including wounded, were evacuated as ships became available. No RAF equipment could be taken, but a few days later a salvage force

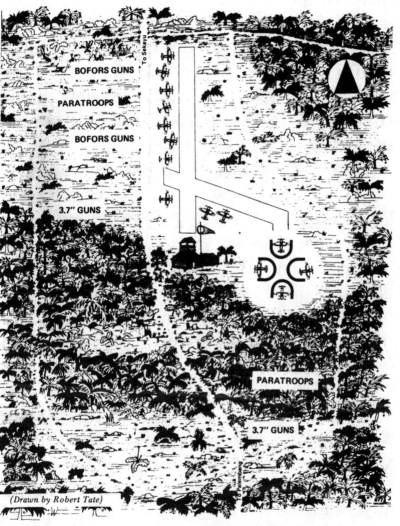

BOFORS GUNS

PARATROOPS

BOFORS GUNS

3.7" GUNS

PARATROOPS

3.7" GUNS

(Drawn by Robert Tate)

P1 Airfield near Palembang where the majority of action and casualties to squadron as a whole incurred. In drawing terminal building artist has allowed himself a little licence! – the building was, in fact, although modest quite a modern one.

returned from Batavia to Oosthaven and salvaged some stores, the remainder being destroyed.

'The PMO Squadron Leader McCarthy, and Squadron MOs worked untiringly throughout the night, and over a long and very difficult road journey, and succeeded in evacuating safely some 35 to 40 wounded and sick.

'The rear guard withdrew in the early hours of February 17th by which time all troops had been got away either to Batavia or Merak in Java.

'Immediately on arrival in Batavia all personnel were placed in barracks and schools. The aircraft continued to operate from Tjillitan until withdrawn to Bandoeng.'

It will be noted that there are certain discrepancies in fact in the above account, as for example that relating to the rearming and refuelling of those landing at P1 but of course as can well be imagined a state of tremendous confusion reigned and continually conflicting accounts were no doubt pouring in. As for the comment about Flying Officer Taute, I met him during the vain attempt of the balance of the 258 pilots to get away from Java, and he never mentioned this — but no doubt by then the minds of none of us were very occupied with what had happened three weeks earlier.

As in the case of 258 Squadron there is a gap in the Operations Record Book for 232 Squadron for the period November 1941 to March 1942 but to some extent this missing period has been filled in by a record written up by the Squadron Adjutant, Flight Lieutenant N. Welch in India at the end of March 1942 with the assistance of Pilot Officer J. K. McKechnie and Sergeant Pilot H. T. Nichols. Part of the entry for February 14th reads:

'The personnel at the aerodrome (P1) were ordered to get back to the town and it was during this that our casualties occurred. Flying Officer H. L. Wright organised a party in one lorry which was mounted with machine guns by the Armourers. There were too many for one lorry so some of the men climbed on a petrol bowser which went on ahead of the lorry. A mile or so down the road they were ambushed, and the petrol bowser overturned blocking the road, trapping and crushing an airman AC1 Kilpatrick H. Another airman AC2 Duff J. L. sustained a broken leg and probably a broken jaw. He was helped to the side of the road while the remainder of the party laboured to lift the bowser and rescue A. C. Kilpatrick. Having no tools or suitable timber this proved difficult, and before it could be accomplished the Japanese attacked in force. Flying Officer Wright was killed and the rest had to take cover. Nothing more was seen of AC Duff. AC Kilpatrick was still alive, and subsequently a Corporal Medical Orderly crawled up under covering fire and injected a double dose of morphia which probably killed him, Meanwhile Flight Sergeant Smith J. A. and Sergeant Ratcliffe L. had been sent on ahead in an army service car used by 3rd Battery Heavy AA. There were army personnel in the car as well, and this car was ambushed by the Japanese, and all the occupants were killed. AC Presdee R. A. was one of a party of unarmed men making their way in single file along the road towards the town. The party was ambushed. He is believed to have lost his life, as nothing is known of him. Leading Aircraftsman Thompson T. E. is a driver MT who was on duty at the aerodrome, and nothing has been heard of him since.

Before finally taking leave of the Japanese paratroops it may be interesting to read an official document headed:

Lessons learnt as a result of Paratroop attack on P1 Palembang, Sumatra.

1. First objective of paratroops is to cut communications. It is therefore vital to have W/T point to somewhere outside particularly when landlines are not buried and can be cut easily.

2. Paratroops are most vulnerable immediately after landing. It is therefore essential that all armed personnel on the aerodrome should be fully mobile to be able to attack the enemy before they consolidate. Had transport been available at P1 very much heavier casualties could have been inflicted on the enemy.

3. AA positions, particularly when outside aerodrome perimeter, are particularly

vulnerable and among the first objectives of paratroops — adequate ground defence should be provided.

4. Armoured cars are essential, particularly for such measures as protecting road approaches and preventing the enemy establishing road blocks.

5. When the aerodrome is located in jungle or heavily wooded country, it is extremely difficult to locate where paratroops land and their position thereafter. Lookout positions in treetops should be arranged, with telephones to main defence headquarters.

6. The most effective way of ascertaining the whereabouts and movements of paratroops in thickly wooded country is by low air reconnaissance in slow type aircraft such as Tiger Moths as the parachutes at least are often visible from the air.

7. The paratroops were armed with Tommy Guns, Machine Guns, Trench Mortars and Hand Grenades. Aerodrome defence arms should include Mortars to return fire over trees and AP light bombs for release from Tiger Moths on paratroop consolidations and Machine

Gun or Mortar posts.

8. The Japanese paratroops at night gave vent to bloodcurdling yells which served three purposes — (1) Consolidation of scattered troops. (ii) Unnerving opponents. (iii) Finding out where opposition was sited as gun and rifle flashes quickly gave away position of posts. It is recommended that the best reply to this is the throwing of hand grenades or the firing of mortars.

9. All pilots should be acquainted with a ground strip code so that the position can be signalled them in the event of attack while they are away from aerodrome and in case W/T or R/T communication breaks down and/or aircraft are not fitted therewith.

10. Steps should be taken to have available means for rapid destruction of all aircraft, equipment etc, in the event of necessity for evacuation. For the destruction of aircraft, petrol tins or drums were placed underneath, petrol cocks of aircraft were turned on and the engine overdoped. A car then proceeded along the line with a rifle and one round of de Wilde ammunition fired into the

tins or drums. Transport should be available. (Unserviceable aircraft should be emptied of all fuel and ammunition to lessen the risk of destruction by fire in the event of an air attack prior to any thoughts of self destruction).

11. Sufficient food, water and ammunition, should be available on the aerodrome in case the aerodrome is cut off, particularly where there is only one approach road to the aerodrome.

12. Where possible arms should be available for all ground personnel and hand grenades should be included. An unarmed man is useless and armed personnel who might be employed for offensive action have to be retained to protect unarmed personnel on the aerodrome.

★ ★ ★

As a glance at the sketch map of P1 makes clear the paratroop drop was superbly planned by the Japanese with one group close to the airfield and the other well positioned for cutting the road to Palembang. Also — although this was possibly due to the fact that a suitable terrain for dropping the troops is so for siting guns, both groups were very near both the 3.7″ and Bofors batteries.

8

Escape to Java

PILOTS who had got to P2 on February 14th spent the night there. At the end of a lane some distance from the airfield there was a hut of some sort and we did the best we could in it sleeping anywhere — on tables, in chairs, on the floor, ravaged by mosquitos and disturbed by thunderstorms. In the morning we were ordered to strafe the invasion barges now proceeding up the River Moesi towards the oil wells and the town.

There were about eight Hurricanes still serviceable and it was arranged that 258 and 232 Squadrons should take turn and turn about on them with 258 making the first attack.

For all the time which has elapsed that day is very clear in my memory because it was a quite remarkable one — in incident just about matching its predecessor.

186

As mentioned earlier, P2 was a vast, sprawling jungle clearing totally hemmed in by jungle and so large that there were even clumps of trees growing in the middle of it which formed no impediment. As we went taxying out looking up I noticed the sky seemed oddly hazy but neither I, nor anyone else, attached any significance to this. It was only when we were airborne, even before our wheels were up, we realised that the haze was a layer of mist which, when broken at two or three hundred feet stretched level, peaceful and white over so far as could be judged the whole thousand miles of Sumatra while as for the airfield, it had simply disappeared.

The American, Art Donahue, who was leading the strike force was the only one to appreciate the danger sufficiently early to avoid it, immediately banging down his undercarriage lever and going down again to land on his take off run.

The problem for the rest of us was a very serious one. There was no method of talking us down and there were no alternative airfields; one had either to land on P2 somehow or take the immediate decision to fly south to Java which was within range which could mean removing the entire and only strike force capable of attacking the invading Japanese. But P2 had quite vanished; it was down there — somewhere; but somewhere is not good enough when what has to be done is to descend through cloud whose base is barely above treetop height. And of course in only moments we would have been completely at sea as to even approximately where the airfield was.

Fortunately Donahue was equal to the moment and hurriedly finding a Very pistol and a supply of cartridges from somewhere he advanced on to the field and started firing upwards through the mist. Through the cloud there suddenly shot a green ball like a bursting Roman Candle and a trail of whitish smoke and at once the Hurricanes, and a single Blenheim presumably intended to guide us to the barges, began to gyrate round it as a centre.

It was a strange business — just the green balls bursting through now and then and the angle of the sun to give an approximate idea of where P2 lay and the rough direction of the landing run.

And it soon became stranger still.

One pilot, like an unenthusiastic swimmer on a winter's day, lowered his flaps and wheels and circumspectly dropped the nose of his Hurricane and disappeared momentarily only almost at once to rear up again in a fierce evasive climb having obviously barely avoided colliding with the trees. And back he came into the circle.

Another tried and either crashed or succeeded in landing because he failed to reappear.

And now instead of seven Hurricanes and a Blenheim there were six Hurricanes and a Blenheim.

There is a blank spot in my mind about that Blenheim. I don't know if he got down on P2 or not. With his longer range the problem would have been a less pressing one to the pilot and being much more cumbersome even than Hurricanes with wheels and flaps down, it was hardly the type of aircraft to attempt what we were obliged to. Probably he hied off to Java — anyway he was quite soon gone leaving just a circle of Hurricanes looking very unreal creeping round with slowly spinning wheels and, some of the time, lowered flaps as well.

I took my turn in an attempted descent and gingerly descended into the woolly depths. For a moment or two all was white and then, suddenly, it was jungle green and I was slamming the throttle open and rearing up again like a startled rabbit into the clear air above. And again I tried and this time found the airfield but instead of travelling along its length I was crossing it diagonally. And so on. I tried at least half a dozen times and couldn't get it quite right although once or twice I did get very near. I was either overshooting, or just to the edge or heading straight for the trees in the middle.

And, meanwhile, depressingly the circle was diminishing in number and I was beginning to ask myself two questions; Would I now have enough petrol to make Kemajoran? And how many Very flares did they have down there? Once they ran out that would be the end of it. I think possibly I would have given it up and while there was a reasonable margin headed off for Java except for my experience in that flight in cloud at Montrose. Then, I told myself, if I had known the aerodrome was just below nothing would have driven me away from it.

So I persevered and, more than that, steeled myself to think intelligently. The first thing — obviously — was to find out the directional bearing of the central axis of this strange shaped jungle airfield. And when you thought about it sensibly that was not too difficult. And you didn't need wheels and flaps down to find it out.

I made a feint with them up and it told me that I wanted — now at least the problem was reduced to one of length and width. How to solve it? The field was very long and relatively narrow because it was waisted in the middle. The dispersal end was wider and the opposite end broadened out considerably giving P2 something of a keyhole shape. It was this which offered a solution.

Uneasily aware that by now there were only a couple more Hurricanes as well as me still trying to get down, I waited for the next rising ball and when it came at once headed for it. Using the smoke it left as a marker point I flew at right angles to what I had figured the longitudinal axis of the airfield would be and started counting. I then turned a right angle and counted off the same number and then a third right angle again counting. If I had it correctly when I turned my fourth right angle I ought to be heading more or less in the right direction for an approach and I ought to have some rough idea how far away P2 was.

Another ball at this juncture would have been very nice but I didn't get it. So I set my course counted off half my number, lowered wheels and flaps and entered the mist.

When I broke through I was a little too much to the right and there were trees below me and I was a little too far along — but nothing was going to have me go up through that lot again. I sideslipped off height to the left which also cleared me from the trees and put me over the landing ground itself, too far along it to avoid running into the jungle at the end but with I believed enough room for manoeuvre. When the field began to open out at the keyhole end, I put on a little right bank to follow its perimeter and then when as near the trees as I dared risk slammed the throttle fully open and brought the stick hard over to the left and back putting the Hurricane into a steep left hand turn. I was of course very low, a matter of fifty feet perhaps. I had wheels and flaps down and of course once into the turn couldn't see the trees I was obviously going to hit if the turn wasn't steep enough; on the other hand I had a clear vision of the airfield in the direction in which I hoped to land. A knot of trees in the middle was an added problem but the really important thing exercising my mind was how steep I dared make my turn without causing an incipient spin. I am satisfied that but for the practice, force majeure, I had had with Wilson in Montrose, I would not have judged it correctly. As it was, I did. I got round the run, took off the bank, got straight, banked a bit again to avoid the knot of trees, straightened up again. I was going very fast but fortunately P2 was long — I fishtailed like mad and it was all right.

The whole exercise had taken forty minutes and two of the precious eight Hurricanes were firmly on their noses on P2. We were down to six.

★ ★ ★

When the weather cleared 232 Squadron took off the remaining aircraft on the original intended mission. They returned about ninety minutes later without loss or damage after encountering as opposition only light fire from the invasion craft. The Hurricanes were quickly refuelled and rearmed for 258.

I flew two to Donahue. He made a prophetic remark.

'Know what I need?' he said to me. 'Just a nick. Just something that'll get me home to an American Squadron now we're in the war.

He was to get his nick — not all that serious, just bad enough to have him sent home to England. He wasn't to get his American Squadron — but he did get a British one. He was to be killed leading it.

★ ★ ★

To deny them to the Japanese, the Dutch had fired the oil wells of Pladjoe. I have read that the weather was bad when we set off on that strafing run but it was not. Had the weather been bad I could not have carried in my mind that clear and awe inspiring picture of those oil wells on fire. The smoke from the refinery rose like a gigantic waterspout but thick, black, oily, palpable.

The smoke rose for several thousand feet before, catching some air current, it spread away like a sign-post, a huge black swathe across the sky pointing to the target and we flew under it as cover. It was a strange atmosphere — above the queer black cloud, below the darkened jungle broken only by the turgid brown swathes of the many rivers which made the Moesi delta. After a time, after perhaps flying for seventy or eighty miles, we came upon small craft, making their way upstream and attacks were made upon them. I found myself in a vertical dive spraying bullets around a small boat. And then it occurred to me to wonder what right I had to assume this held Japanese, that for all I knew it might be a boat packed with natives escaping the invaders. I packed it in. In any case it was a futile exercise, sledgehammers cracking nuts. Twelve Brownings against a fishing boat — it wasn't what 232 had talked about.

I kept close to Donahue and he was puzzled too, looking this way and that.

And then we came upon the barges.

There was a string of them heading upstream keeping in close to the northern bank, presumably searching for such cover as the currents and shallows allowed. They were large barges packed with men like sardines in a tin and because at this point the river ran straight they were in a long straight line. It is difficult to estimate how many men each barge contained but probably it would have been two hundred. Their sole defence was a machine gunner mounted in each — I really can't remember if it was in the prow or stern — and the soldiers gave the impression of being so tightly packed they couldn't have raised their arms to fire at us. It was a remarkable sight. The barges, except for a thin white streak like a tail in the rear of each stirring the brown of the river white, seemed motionless and they made a curious spectacle these oblongs of upturned faces.

It was carnage.

Each Hurricane had a fire power of about 12,000 rounds a minute with a total loading of about 4,000 rounds and the guns were not loaded merely with normal bullets used by infantry but with a leavening of what is used in air warfare — armour piercing, tracer and incendiary. The target was to all practical purposes helpless.

I probably saw the effect of Donahue's attack much better than any of my own because I had fallen astern behind him waiting my turn and with nothing to do and not much to think about but watch.

The flicker of the defending gunners was like torches switched on and off but no more than that. We had orbited to get straight in line and dived from perhaps a thousand feet. I really don't believe Donahue missed a barge, his guns raking the convoy from head to stern. The bullets made an unforgettable pattern. There was a pincushion of water ahead of the nearest barge which moved along so that as the bullets raked through a barge what one saw was the pinpoints of light in the barge itself which would have been the tracers striking and the pincushioning carrying along both sides of the barges and then reappearing in between each barge. And so on along the line.

It is impossible to conceive the horror and the slaughter wrought. Later even the Japanese were to talk of it in awe. When we were taken prisoner we took off and destroyed our brevets because we believed that had the Japanese in our camp known we were the pilots who had strafed them on the Moesi they would have taken their revenge.

Donahue made the single effective run because he got a bullet in his leg from one of the machine gunners; I saw him break away and head off back to P2. I stayed a little longer and was unharmed.

By the time I landed at P2 Donahue had already been taken off for treatment.

There were many things about the war in the Dutch East Indies I never understood but of them all perhaps the most incomprehensible was the fact that we were not ordered to repeat the attacks on the barges. Two strafes had been made and no Hurricanes had been lost; there was so far as I know ample petrol and ammunition for six Hurricanes at P2. The Japanese had been we were sure, and as was afterwards to be confirmed, brutally weakened if not as yet stopped. It is not at all impossible, that a couple more strikes would have stopped them in their tracks. And defeat if only temporary in Sumatra would have made the invasion of Java infinitely more difficult and perhaps put some spirit into the Dutch.

But 258 at least, I can't answer for 232, made no more strikes; instead we were told to get away as best we could to Java. It really was extraordinary. There couldn't possibly have been a Japanese within fifty miles of P2 and in fact they didn't by that time even know of its existence.

Before we were told to get away we sat around, Lambert, Sheerin, Scott, me and a couple of others watching rather gloomily an impressive oil fire somewhere near at hand. Presumably that would have been petrol storage tanks on fire. There was a terrible general atmosphere of depression and defeat; much the same as in Singapore and yet in a way more tangible. One almost expected Japanese suddenly to rush us from the jungle. We ate tinned sausages and wondered what was going to happen next — we hadn't any Hurricanes. Others had taken them. I don't know who. Then came the casual, weary order that we were on our own.

We walked down the lane which led to the airfield. A rutted sort of track with low thick bushes on either hand. We knew quite well there weren't any enemy in miles but we still felt uneasy.

The track came to a T-junction. To the left it led to the railway station and the road to Palembang, to the right to the airfield.

We held a council of war — which way

to go. Bertie and I were for the airfield, there might be Hurricanes which could be made serviceable — one would do for two pilots; one sitting in the other's lap. It had been done before. Sheerin and Scott were for the railway.

These were the decisions made; and it was quite remarkable how our lives were changed.

Sheerin and Scott made their way down to the southern tip of Sumatra and escaped by boat. They must have separated en route for Sheerin got to Australia via Java where after spending nine months with 22 Squadron he was reposted as Chief Flying Instructor of fighter pilots at some New South Wales station, while Scott boarded a ship at Oosthaven whose captain was wise enough not to permit him to land when it docked, briefly, at Tandjeonpriok near Batavia. His end was tragic. Like Micky Nash, Scott was to fly continuously in Burma, often in action, rising to the rank of Flying Officer. On January 11th 1944, less than a month after Micky Nash had been killed in a flying accident he was to lose his life in the same sort of way.

With another Flying Officer he was detailed to escort a VIP from Chittagong to Ramu; while waiting they decided to fill in their time practising ciné gun attacks on each other. Scott completed his and the other Flying Officer began his own but, accidentally pressing his gun button in error for his ciné gun, he shot down Scott and killed him.

* * *

On the airfield we found to our glee, and surprise, two Hurricanes one of which was none other, Number 5481, than the one in which I had made all of my flights over the past two days. Now it was unserviceable so perhaps 232 had made another strike — or perhaps another pilot getting away to Java had damaged it in a rut taxying out and changed to another.

The problem seemed to be connected with the tail wheel.

'Can't fly that one, sarge', a loyal ground staff grunted. 'Never get it off.'

'How d'you know?'

'Someone tried to. Went careering to

the left like mad. Stopped just in time. Just short of the rubber. Death trap.'

I looked across the all but deserted field. Bertie was already clambering into the cockpit of the second Hurricane. I never discovered the saga of that one, or if I did I've long since forgotten it. But it very much looked as if Bertie had found what he was hoping for; if we were going to try the two in one idea, one sitting on the other's lap, I'd have to hurry. I made my mind up.

'I'm going to try in this,' I told the ground staff.

'You'll kill yourself,' a sergeant said succinctly.

I climbed up and into the cockpit. Bertie from across the airfield put his thumb up in relief and I saw his propeller start to turn. The die was cast now that he'd reassured himself I didn't need help from him; to be the last of 258 pilots left behind on an empty aerodrome was an unimaginable possibility.

I checked the one vital gauge. The tank was full. I nodded to the sergeant who shrugged and ordered the aircraft started. Probably he didn't mind too much — when it had gone or crashed, there'd be nothing left to keep him here.

The engine coughed and started, the turning propeller became a misty circle tipped with colour at its rim. I held up a thumb and the chocks were hauled away. Bertie was already taxying across to the south end of the airfield. I taxied after him — or at least started to. But the sound below was awesome, the sensation horrible — like driving a car with the back wheels missing and everything scraping on the road — and there was a frightful yawing to the left.

The men came ambling over and the sergeant shouted something I couldn't hear — 'What did I tell you?' I imagine.

I shouted down and signalled for them to turn me round at a diagonal to the take off run, helping them with rudder and a touch of throttle, then waved them away and goodbye. There was a lot going for being a pilot. I saw Bertie begin his take off run, disappear past me then come into sight again already unstuck and his undercarriage going up. I felt envious.

I checked everything and let down the flaps a shade to give added lift, kept the brakes on and opened up the throttle as wide as I dared without tipping the Hurricane on its nose, then let go the brakes and slammed the throttle open. At once the Hurricane lurched away yawing horribly and with a frightful rending sound in an arc to port yet gaining speed. The jungle horizon began turning clockwise at a sickening rate and there was a juddering vibration in the whole machine. Then suddenly that was gone as I unstuck but the jungle had gone as well and in its place ahead of me was a black wooden hut I hadn't even noticed before almost on the perimeter — I was at ninety degrees to take off direction. It wasn't a very big hut but it was big enough to hit and I was sure I was going to. But I hauled back on the stick and scraped over somehow, cleared the surrounding jungle and tore off after Bertie.

We got to Kemajoran safely, beat it up and landed. I kept the tail up as long as I dared and the speed down as low as possible and landed on the right side of the runway. It wasn't too bad — I slewed off but without any damage. Whatever the trouble was it couldn't have been too bad because the next day I was able to ferry the same machine to nearby Tjillitan for operational duties.

Pip Healey we'd given up for lost in Singapore was in a cinema and heard us land. He was at Kemajoran before we quit it.

Meanwhile the balance of 258 Squadron pilots, that is to say those who had not escaped from P2 either by Hurricane or by making their way southwards, in other words those in Palembang itself, moved fast. They commandeered a launch, filled it with provisions, arms and spare cans of petrol and set off up river on the Moesi ahead of the invasion barges, then in turn made their way down to Oosthaven on the Southern tip and crossed by boat to Java. The party included Macnamara and Red Campbell who, bless him, made the time to go through the sergeants quarters collecting all the personal items he considered they might think particularly valuable — including Log Books! I got mine back in Java.

At the end of this account I have explained that, apart from the exceptions noted, it has been written from recollection with no attempt to seek material from surviving 258 Squadron pilots. But after the draft was done I happened, through my search for photographs, to hear from Arthur Sheerin who escaped to his home country, Australia where he went on to help form No 77, Kittyhawk Squadron before being posted to a Senior Flying Training School as Instructor on Wirraways for fifteen months and then, finally, with the rank of Flight Lieutenant, Acting Squadron Leader, to test and ferry flying.

As a matter of fact, having apparently forgotten we have summer time, he telephoned me at five o'clock one morning delighted to hear after thirty five years that I was in the land of the living, as was I about him, and followed this by sending me a batch of photographs used in this book and an account of his experiences from the time when he got away from P2 and I found his letter so delightful as to want to quote from it verbatim. For the sake of chronology I have split the quoted passages into two parts which follow each other without break the first of which follows now and the balance later. I have learnt from this letter several things — that Arty — or Artie as he calls himself — was probably in the first sixteen who took off from *Indomitable* because he was up flying in Singapore, that it was he who with the help of some engineers pulled Roy Keedwell from his burning Hurricane and that he too was flying on that vexing occasion before we strafed the paratroops when we lost sight of P2 because of cloud — whether he strafed or whether his was one of the two Hurricanes which ended on their noses, I do not know.

His letter reads:

'You will recall we were getting desperate for aircraft and six of us were flown in a Dutch Loadstar to Batavia for replacements (at *very* low level). We picked them up and led by 'Hutch'[1] flew back to P1 over

---

[1] I do not know who "Hutch" was — possibly a 232 Squadron pilot.

cloud all the way. Hutch got lost
and decided to descend and have a
look — you can imagine our surprise
when he lobbed us fair in the middle
of a formation of Zeros and bombers
dropping paratroops. One word was
said: "God, go like bloody hell" as we
had no ammo nor fuel — there was a
surry of Hurricanes headed for the trees
— I thought I was good at low flying
but some guy passed underneath me
going in the opposite direction. Another
chap, I think "Scotty", landed at P1
and was waved off by one of our chaps
with curtains off the terminal. It was
a *record* turnaround. Some made P2
but I think three of us pranged — at
least I did. I was hightailing it through
the trees "Nil" fuel on the gauge when
three Zeros pounced on me.

Having slipped them the engine
stopped and it was then the jungle
or the river. (Mousie, I think)[1] I took
the latter and according to the manual
on ditching the flaps should have come

---

[1] River Moesi

off on impact. Well they didn't — I did three beautiful take offs and (on) the final landing I sank like a stone. After drinking half the river I surfaced, got into the dinghy[1] and made the bank, found a native fire going but no "bods". After a while they did emerge — I told them in some stupid "lingo" I wanted to get to the "Big Town" or village and *fast* as the place by this time was full of paratroops.

They in turn took me to another village who had a boat. We then set off down the river for Palembang. After some time, out of the vines on the bank came a speedboat with Dutch Naval blokes all taking a bead on me with their guns thinking, I suppose, I was a Jap paratroop. Standing up, shouting, I tipped our boat over and was picked up by the Dutch and

---

[1] The dinghy fixed underneath a pilot's parachute and easily inflated. Earlier McCulloch's launching of his dinghy and paddling through a swamp has been recounted.

taken back to the bank whence they had come from and was surprised to see hidden under the bushes etc quite a large ship which was stuck due to the Japs having taken Palembang city.[1] Further surprise the Captain took me to his mess for a Scotch and there was, I think, Red Campbell who had also been shot down.[2]

The Dutch then agreed to take us as near to Palembang as possibly safe. When we got there it was a shambles — panic, everyone trying to get away. I got across the river on a punt and having spotted a staff car with a very frightened LAC driver at the wheel asked him what he was waiting for. His reply: "My Commanding Officer." My reply: "You stupid B . . . let's get out of here" and jumped in. We then drove to P2.

You will know what happened there, no doubt. As to my escape from P2 you were correct. I remember "Scotty"

---

[1] Which, of course, they hadn't by then.
[2] This ties up well with author's account

and someone else setting off by foot. I went back to the aerodrome and some chap asked me if I could fly a Blenheim as he pointed to one and said it was full of chaps awaiting a driver. At that stage I would have flown anything so I said "yes". On my way to the aircraft I noticed in the bushes (a Hurricane) minus a tail wheel — that's for me! So in I got, started up, popping and smoking and commenced to taxi on the rudder when a Flt/Lt duty pilot jumped on the wing and shouted "That's mine. I hid it there." One thing to do, says Artie, blow him off, which I did. As I commenced my take off run Japs were on the end of the drome and firing at me.[1] I lost no time heading *very low* for Batavia with my popping Hurricane and a map on a cigarette case to navigate by. Later to land in safety.'

_____

[1] This doesn't tie in!

9

Days of Wine and Roses

THE philosophy of the Dutch Colonial was quite different from that of his British counterpart who, while enthusiastic enough to make his *career* in some far flung outpost of Empire carried retirement images of green fields and sleepy hamlets. To a Dutchman home was where he spent his working life and where he spent his working life was usually the place in which he died. Leaving Holland young he would take the first steps up the rungs of an overseas career before going back to find himself a wife and taking her back with him, probably never to return.

In consequence the quality of life in a Dutch possession was of a far better order with towns planned for living in rather than as places in which to get things done, as communities rather than administration centres. The clubs were there, but less important — the homes, delightful.

Even Palembang, a mere oil town cut from a swampy, foetid jungle had considerable quality. And Batavia was a paradise — a garden city of fine hotels, outstanding restaurants, sophisticated night clubs, air conditioned shops, broad streets, flowers, blossom, bustle, noise and colour.

And we were rich. Millionaires.

No 258 Squadron ground staff having at long last arrived by ship on February 14th were, on the evacuation of Sumatra, promptly and sensibly shipped off again to India in favour of the ground staff of 605 Squadron who had come out earlier on the Warwick Castle and were already more experienced. In consequence the imprest fund intended for a unit of several hundred men was available to meet the daily needs of hardly more than a dozen pilots who might all within a week or two be dead or prisoners.

If you wanted money you asked for it and it was peeled from a wad of guilders — for the first time in our lives, everything was free.

We had a splendid time. The first thing to do was to re-equip and so for the third time we went shopping but this time to the best bespoke tailors along the Rijswijk who could kit you out to measure in twenty four hours. We frequented splendid hotels, the Hotel der Nederlanden, the Hotel des Indes and drank the new fad, highballs. The relief of escaping from Singapore and Sumatra and the awareness one's luck mightn't hold out for ever gave life tremendous sharpness.

Driven like lords in bicycle rickshaws along the teeming streets, ambling along the Mowlenvliet, leaning on the wall to the canal down the centre of the Rijswijk listening to the kopteks croaking — (if it croaked seven times that was supposed to mean a death) — eyeing the girls, spending money like profligates we would airily discuss the evening's programme. Should we for once forsake the Capitool for dinner at Harmony House; should we slum it later and instead of seeing dawn up in the Black Cat head for one of the open dance halls where the bats flew across the floor and the taxi girls sat around in dozens. But mostly this was talk. Invariably we ate at the Capitool and almost invariably it was the Black Cat afterwards.

At the Capitool you ate mixed grills. I have never before or since seen such gargantuan meals as the Dutch ate in Java. We ordered one mixed grill to do for two of us, not because the cost was of account, but because even one between two was more than could be managed. A mixed grill in Batavia consisted of two steaks, two pork chops, two lamb cutlets, two veal schnitzels, kidneys, sausages and sweetbreads; and accompanying it were nine inch diameter tureens of fried potatoes, peas, carrots, beans, nasigoreng and other new and as yet unnamed vegetables and dishes. We did our best treating it as a challenge, tucking in like trenchmen and washing it all down with great mugs of light Dutch beer and enjoying every moment. The Capitool was ideally situated at the end of the Rijswijk where it turned sharply slowing the traffic, a covered restaurant with open sides through which we could watch life seething past: cars, bicycles, rickshaws and pedestrians; Europeans, Malays in brilliant sarongs, Chinese. And nearer at hand, calming the hooting the ringing and the shouting, music in the restaurants.

The Capitool was, I suppose, the premier restaurant in Java, difficult to beat throughout the East. I imagine the well-dressed Dutch businessmen with their women found us noisy and inconsiderate, callow, brash and over self-contained; considered that we drank, and joked and laughed too much; that we were something of an intrusion. But we wore pilots' brevets on our tunics and we were fighting the Japanese which was more than either they were doing or intended to and so they made no objections — and even, occasionally in passing, put a hand on our shoulders and quite unnecessarily insisted on paying our bill.

The atmosphere was odd. The Dutch in Java had quite accepted that the Japanese would soon invade and occupy their country. They talked quite openly of it and I never remember hearing any of them suggest the Japanese could be repulsed. Yet this was an island eight hundred miles in length with a population of sixty million. It didn't seem to cross their minds that the hugeness of Java with its mountains and jungles, its myriad rivers, its capacity for supporting numberless small groups of men, its tremendous coastline, its many towns, airfields, ports, could have provided the background of a bloody resistance to an enemy already stretched too far. They just sat around and waited for the Japanese to come.

A few, but very few, made an effort to escape — the majority did not. The few of them who talked about it explained that this was their home and they had nowhere else to go and, I think, assumed that so long as they behaved themselves and weren't too much of a nuisance the Japanese would leave them alone. This is exactly what the Japanese did, at first — it was convenient for them to have the administration of the country carried on more or less intact while they were looting it. The Dutch were desperately anxious lest their beautiful towns should be destroyed — the Japanese only too pleased to accommodate them. And this curious pact had already been agreed between the businessmen tucking in each evening in the Capitool and the Japanese getting together their tiny invasion fleet.

After the leisurely two hour dinner in the Capitool we would normally head for the Black Cat which was a night club of remarkable quality with one of the largest bars and one of the best and largest dance bands I ever met with in such a place. In London the Regent Palace Hotel in Piccadilly was the recognised meeting place for pilots on leave; in Batavia the Black Cat had a similar role. First arrivals would reserve several tables by sitting thinly at a couple and laying revolvers in holsters which it had been decreed we should always wear, on others. By the time the evening was well on we would be packing several tables and others would be piled with armaments. We ordered incredible rounds of highballs and sooner or later the whole squadron, or what was by then left of it, would rise somewhat tipsily to its feet and regale the other customers with the 258 Squadron song with actions.

This was called 'To you sweetheart
   — Aloha' —
'To you, sweetheart, Aloha.
Aloha from the bottom of my heart
Keep that smile on your lips
Wipe that tear from your eyes,
One more Aloha
And it's time for goodbyes.
To you, sweetheart — Aloha
In dreams I'll be with you dear tonight
And I'll pray for that day — when
We two shall meet again
Until then
Sweetheart,
Alohaaaaaaaaaa.'

The actions of course fitted the words
and were carried out with the perfect
timing of much practice in every bar
and pub in England where 258 Squadron
had foregathered and started drinking.
On the whole I don't think the rest of
the people in the various establishments
minded — such goings on were part of
the wartime scene. Nowadays you'd get
thrown out.

The song was, obviously, of New
Zealand extraction; it's a sad thought

220

to reflect how few of the original New Zealanders who used to sing it survived the war.

Apart from drinking and singing squadron songs one was interested in women and if one was fortunate there were very beautiful girls to know in Java. I met such a one — her name was Julie and after the war I called my first car after her. She used to wear glittering sequined evening dresses with glittering sequined skull caps to match. She was a truly lovely creature with wonderful dark eyes, a husky voice, a superb and memorable body and was sophisticated beyond the wildest dreams of a boy of twenty-one. She used to join me at the Black Cat after finishing her voluntary work at the Holland Huis where I had met her and even my CO used to ask my permission to dance with her.

We, the sergeant pilots, now fell properly on our feet having had made available to us a splendid private house, fully staffed and owned by a Naval reservist who had been called up and got his wife and family away to another house he owned near Bandoeng. We saw him just the once when he took us round, showed us where the drinks and cigars were kept, handed us the keys, wished us luck and told us that if we wanted to get away he was hoping at the end to escape in his yacht and there would be places for us.

When the time came we forgot all about him — but I don't suppose that signified. If he hadn't already got away by then, he probably didn't anyway.

We had issued to us a Bedford Van which we used to park on his front lawn and in which we used to drive to Tjillitan when on readiness.

They were golden days those last two weeks in Batavia. To have the contrast of exciting days and luxurious nights — to be young and have the stamina to manage both. To be rich, to have companionship of every kind, to be in a new and thrilling country and to value every hour of every day . . . one cannot ask for more.

10

The Final Flights

ON February 18th, Number 226 Group was formally disbanded becoming part of what came to be known as West Group to which Air Commodore Vincent was transferred together with the Staff Officers of 226 Group. Although the pilots generally were not as yet to know of it the decision had been taken to reduce the fighter squadrons to two, 242 and 605, with all surplus personnel being evacuated from the country. The full details relating to this decision are set down in the *History of 226 Group* which does however contain an important omission in that it indicates that all the 258 Squadron pilots were got out which as will be seen was not the case. It correctly states that the pilots of 232 were transferred en bloc to 242 Squadron to commence flying operationally from

Tjillitan. This statement may appear to convey that 232 Squadron pilots were an addition to those of 242. This was not so — 242 Squadron had no pilots, only ground staff fresh out from U.K.; thus so far as air crews are concerned any reference anywhere to 242 Squadron really means 232.

There were twenty-five pilots of 232 of which two, Squadron Leader Wright posted to command and Pilot Officer Hutton, were transferred to 605 Squadron. This wealth of pilots may seem strange considering that 232 had seen so much action in Singapore and Sumatra but it must be remembered that originally the squadron had forty-eight pilots, the twenty-four who came out on the convoy which docked at Singapore on January 13th and the twenty-four who flew off the *Indomitable* two weeks later. Thus to date their wastage from one cause or another had been twenty three as compared with nine of 258. Nevertheless twenty-three, being the number now attached to 242, was a lot of pilots and far more than there were Hurricanes to fly — the maximum number of Hurricanes ever becoming available in Java on any one day being in fact eighteen, with this number quite exceptional and the normal tally between six and twelve.

It could have been more. There were available in Java a further twenty-four Hurricanes which had been handed over to the Dutch Air Force at their request which, so far as anybody knew they had never flown operationally and were never to fly operationally, and which they obstinately refused to return and were, presumably either destroyed or captured by the Japanese unused.

However the best had to be made of a bad job and if there was a lamentable lack of aircraft at least strenuous efforts could be made to improve on the conditions under which we had operated in Sumatra.

As is stated by Air Commodore Vincent:

A very satisfactory Operations Room was operating within a week. A filter room was completed and operating within ten days. The Ops Room was complete with a large scale 'table' together with telephones to three aerodromes, R/T communication with aircraft, observer corps liaison, communication with gun and search-light positions and direct lines to Bandoeng and Sourabaya. In addition the filter room was connected up to two R.D.F. sets and two G.L. sets and three small American sets were being sited but were never actually in use. A W/T set was kept for work with HMS *Exeter*, from whom much useful information was obtained on several occasions and a W/T point between the Ops Room and Tjilititang (Tjillitan) and Tjisaoek (the P2 of Tjillitan) laid on.

Thus, late in the day, a substantial effort was being made to put the meagre fighter defence of the final glittering prize yet outstanding to the Japanese, into some sort of shape. It was a noble effort but it could not undo the shocking errors of the past four weeks — it could merely help to delay the enemy and to little purpose for, with only the most isolated of exceptions, the Dutch had no will to fight and no intention of doing so.

★ ★ ★

During the third week in February it was announced that 258 Squadron was to be withdrawn from Java with the proviso that six of its pilots should stay behind. These, together with six pilots from 488 Squadron which had arrived in Singapore as early as October and had taken, in their much outclassed Brewster Buffaloes, the brunt of the first Japanese attacks, were to form a new 605 Squadron under Squadron Leader Wright DFM who had risen from sergeant pilot to flight lieutenant and then been promoted squadron leader on the death of the original commanding officer of 232 — Squadron Leader Llewellin who had been killed when he hit a wireless mast when taking off from Kallang. The new 605 (originally the County of Warwickshire Auxiliary Squadron with as its emblem the bear and ragged staff) was to fly from Tjillitan.

In order to select which six should stay behind it was arranged that all remaining pilots of 258 would meet one morning at the Hotel des Indes, a beautiful flower embowered hotel facing the splendid Rijswijk.

The 258 pilots present at this meeting were:

Thomson, Harry Dobbyn, Ambrose Milnes, Victor de la Perelle, Bertie Lambert, Micky Nash, Campbell White, Red Campbell, Pip Healey, McCulloch, Arty Sheerin and myself. In addition five other pilots were present who had arrived on the scene (in some cases rather mysteriously) including a pearl handled pistol packing American named Cicurel, and nicknamed Cy, who must have been very rich for he had in Palembang, I was told, rented the whole floor of an hotel to ensure himself a good night's sleep. There was also amongst them a New Zealand sergeant pilot named Vibert.

Thomson explained the situation: that six pilots must stay out of the fifteen who remained after he and Nash had been excluded; of these one, whom he nominated — Harry Dobbyn — would be appointed flight commander of 'A' Flight which was to be composed entirely of pilots of 258. For the other five he called first for volunteers. Campbell and Vibert obliged, leaving three out of the balance of twelve still required. It was decided to cut cards and this was done out on the verandah facing the Rijswijk, watching the traffic passing by, sipping highballs.

In such manner are the lives of men changed.

I happened to be nearest to Thomson when cards were handed to him. He held out the pack — I took the topmost card: the six of diamonds. Bertie Lambert drew the two of clubs and Pip Healey another low one. Practically all the others' cuts were high, picture cards proliferating.

Thus, suddenly, the rump of 258 was cut into two further sections: those who would escape; and those who would stay.

And 'A' Flight was to consist of two officers, Dobbyn and Campbell, and four sergeant pilots, Lambert, Healey, Vibert and myself.

★ ★ ★

This seems a convenient place in which to quote the balance of Arthur Sheerin's letter of which the first part has been included in an earlier chapter. It is quite certain that unless I was flying that day I would have seen Arthur and Campbell White off at Batavia station and I am pretty sure that in the photograph, I am talking to him and Teddy Tremlett who was to be killed when flying against the Japanese when they attacked Colombo Harbour on April 5th.

The balance of the letter to be quoted read:

'Now for Java. We stayed with a Dutch Naval Officer. (Sherperes or something)[1] and usually dined at a place run by a Dutch woman called as pronounced "Tenner-a-bang" where we discussed our operations.[2] Once again short on aircraft. I remember us trying to bargain rather heatedly with

---

[1] This would be the reservist referred to in account.
[2] Unless there were two places I think this must have been the Hotel Der Nederlanden as cards were certainly cut in a hotel. I thought it was the Hotel des Indes.

Americans for use of their Kittyhawks as they were too scared to fly — this did not work.

'Can you recall all those Hurricanes parked in streets under trees *but no wings*? Typical Air Force; the wings were on another ship which had been sunk.

'I think we all knew we had "had it" and the final meeting with Thomson one morning at "Tenner-a-bang". (*See previous footnote.*) I remember him saying that we had six aircraft left and that a signal from Air Ministry had stated we must fly to the last man and machine. We would draw cards "Ace High". Six must stay — the rest, what was left of us, could escape the best way we could. Yes, Terry, I drew the ace.

'Cam White and I set off for the railway which was teeming with Navy, Army and Air Force as we discovered this was the only and last train for Tjilatjap. What a trip, the engine ran out of fuel so — what to do? Chop up the seats or anything! Just let us get cracking!

'We finally reached the port — which was in utter confusion with people shouting, yelling and *PANIC*. I bumped two Quantas flying boat captains, Captain Bateman and Captain Connelly who were about to depart for Darwin — Bateman begged me to come with him but I would not leave Cam — it is thought they ran into the Jap Navy.

'We scrambled on to a small (about 3/4000 tons) ship not knowing where we were going. It was so packed with troops there was no room to move at night. The chaps would tie themselves to the rail to sleep. No hope of stretching out. Cam and I used to get next to the funnel to keep warm as all we had was what we had on — safari jacket, shorts and flying boots — as a matter of fact I still had "Kleck's"[1] blood on my tunic after we had picked him up in the jungle in Sumatra. No food except a piece of tinned cheese and one cup of water a day. Quite a few died

---

[1] The American, Cardell Kleckner.

on the trip with simple fever[1] — the Doc worked endlessly — but had no medical supplies.

'After seven days we landed in Ceylon harbour. Straight to the Gall Face Hotel where we met quite a few of the chaps we knew including Thomson.

We had one scrap there with the Japs then Thomson called a meeting and informed us we could go our own ways. I saw a British ship in the harbour, the *Stirling Castle* due to leave immediately for direct voyage unescorted to Melbourne Australia. When I pointed this out to Thomson he said "Go to it and good luck". Just in time I boarded her and off. We took a course straight down to the South Pole and then up to Melbourne — can you imagine me still in my summer togs!

'On arrival in Melbourne we were given about £20 and straight off home in all directions by rail. I arrived in

---

[1] Probably dengue fever.

Sydney Easter Sunday and was pulled up by a service police who must have thought I was bats — blood stained tunic, shorts and flying boots with my pith helmet. I can assure you, Terry, they were well and truly told in my best language.'

Tjillitan had two runways which met to form an 'L' and from any height this gash which exposed blood red earth in green fertile land was an unfailing landmark to friend and foe alike; it lay perhaps thirty minutes from Batavia.

242 Squadron originally operated with twelve Hurricanes. 605 operated with six Hurricanes in two flights each of six pilots, and adopted a system whereby one flight would fly from lunchtime on one day until lunchtime on the next and have the following twenty four hours free. It was the best arrangement giving the pilots twenty-four hours of intense excitement followed by the blissful relief of a whole day released from duty.

There were two readiness huts — attractive thatched affairs with verandahs where easy chairs were supplied for pilots on readiness. Inside each hut was a telephone both for normal communication and for combat instructions. The 605 readiness hut was just south of the east/west runway close to where this met the north/south runway and the 242 readiness hut was on the edge of the north/south runway and close to it. Behind the east/west runway towards its western end were modern buildings now depressingly deserted with their windows smashed and their lavatories choked with filth. I never remember seeing any Dutchmen and no attempt was ever made to clean up these buildings or put the lavatories into a decent state. The whole thing was quite disgusting.

From a flying point of view things were far better than they had been in Sumatra. Apart from the operations room now running well, there were to the north, on the myriad islands in the Sunda Straits, watchers who reported the approach of enemy aircraft. Thus, for the first time, there was fair warning and the chance of climbing high enough to engage the enemy if not in equal numbers, at least otherwise on reasonable terms.

The Japanese attacked daily and in the same sort of strength which seemed to mark their general pattern: a bomber formation escorted by upwards of forty Navy 0s. The Hurricanes started flying at Tjillitan from about February 18th and in spite of being continually outnumbered at the beginning many times and latterly as aircraft were lost more disproportionately still, and in spite of their airfield being continually bombed and strafed, maintained a useful resistance until about March 3rd and at least a presence from another airfield, Andir, until Java fell on March 8th.

The reasons for this were twofold: growing experience in the pilots and reasonable warning. If anything proved the Maguire approach correct it was Tjillitan. Indeed had the Maguire approach been followed we should have had the remarkable experience of outnumbering the Japanese, and being invariably in the most favourable combat situation.

A force of what might well have been a hundred fighters operating from several airfields with a planned system of operations and working with a respectable bombing force would have presented the Japanese with their absurdly stretched communications with problems they had met with neither in their advance down Malaya, nor, with the possible exception of the Philippines, in any other field. All the advantages would have been with the Hurricanes.

One of the big problems facing the Luftwaffe during the Battle of Britain was that the Messerschmitts had to fly long distances to and back from the field of operations and damaged aircraft could not be put down quickly on home based airfields nor shot down pilots recovered; exactly the same conditions would have applied to the Japanese who could only have attacked from Palembang several hundred miles to the north or from vulnerable aircraft carriers operating in an area subject to sudden and fierce tropical storms. Sumatra could have been a nasty thorn in the side of the Japanese but Java might have held. It was the one possible base for operations on a grand scale granted time to prepare; fought for tenaciously it had the size and terrain to absorb reverses; its southern coast was never for long a Japanese sea. A spirited air of resistance which would have been apparent to the native troops who fought with varying degrees of courage and to the Dutch who never, with the honourable exception of their Navy, fought at all might have helped build a different attitude.

The key lay in the air and in the air the Japanese fighters although of a quality which surprised the Allies were not machine for machine superior to the Hurricane when handled by pilots who had learnt their craft against the Navy 0. Much has been written to say they were but much of this is apologia. Full data are available for those sufficiently interested to compare performance in many manuals written on the subject (which manuals incidentally confirm that the total number of Navy 0s delivered by the outbreak of the Japanese war was only 400 and that they did not possess the hordes erroneously assumed.) The Navy 0s advantages were that it was at certain heights (up to about 20,000 feet) slightly faster and it had a definite advantage in manoeuvrability.

But it was unarmoured, its fire power was less, its ceiling was apparently lower (we never saw a Navy 0 operating above 30,000 feet) and, above all, it lacked the astonishing capacity of the Hurricane to absorb punishment.

Another favourable factor, mentioned earlier, was the very discipline of the Japanese air force which enabled one, once the tactics were understood, to cope with it. Apart from the war at sea the only real opposition to the Japanese invading Java came from the Hurricanes — it should have been the simplest matter with such an advantage in numbers to have kept continual small patrols of Navy 0s over Tjillitan and thus prevent us landing. So far as I was concerned at least, not once did I meet enemy aircraft on returning to base even though the field had been bombed and strafed while we were absent. Again, as Healey was to underline, captains of ships such as the *Empire Star* on which he escaped from Singapore soon learnt that the risk of destruction under air attack was amazingly reduced by the simple expedient of only altering course when the bomb doors were seen to open in the knowledge that all bombs would invariably be dropped together. And equally the pilots of 232 and 258, and of 488 when at last after their hopeless Buffaloes they were given worthwhile tools, learnt, if too late to be of significance, how what had seemed insoluble was manageable.

Had a substantial force of enemy bombers been attacked by a force of Hurricanes of sufficient size to detach a part equal in number to the defending fighters and had those Hurricanes been flown by pilots with combat experience, acting to a thought out plan with reliable intercommunication between air and ground and air and air, the most dreadful havoc could have been wrought. But such was not to be. Never once in Malaya, Singapore, Sumatra, Borneo, Celebes, Bali, Timor or Darwin did such a situation obtain.

But at least, at Tjillitan, some of the drawbacks had been overcome.

The initial losses of 258 Squadron, now become 'A' Flight of 605 Squadron, occurred on the second scramble.

We had discussed tactics at great depth and knowing that we might quite often expect sufficient warning to be above the Japanese had decided that the thing to do was to adopt a dive and climb policy. We would fly up to maximum altitude — about thirty four thousand feet — await the arrival of the Japanese, dive down on them having one long burst en route and whether successful or not keep going straight down knowing after the Palembang experience that the Navy 0s even if they could keep pace with us wouldn't be able to stay because they would disintegrate on pull out. We would then pull out and climb up again when well clear to repeat the exercise. These were not of course the most exciting of tactics but they were we believed those best calculated to keep a fighter presence and more importantly to stay alive. We would not score many victories perhaps, we would probably not even know when we had scored victories, but at least we would be an infernal nuisance to the enemy.

On the second scramble there were only five of us, the sixth Hurricane presumably temporarily out of service. We got to our thirty odd thousand feet and after a while, sure enough, the Japanese were below circling in two concentric rings one several thousand feet below the other. There was Harry Dobbyn, Red Campbell, Bertie Lambert, Vibert[1] and me. We peeled off to attack — Harry Dobbyn, followed by one of the sergeants, then Campbell and the other two. I selected my own target and started firing at him from a long way off, staying with the one I picked so far as possible by the use of aileron and rudder. It isn't as easy as it sounds. To start with at thirty four thousand feet a Hurricane is wallowing in thin air and there's not much precision either in the beginning or the passage of a dive — and of course the Japanese sees you coming and takes evasive action. On the other hand a tropical sun is pretty vertical and it's difficult to look into. At all events I

---

[1] I have subsequently heard from Vibert he was not flying that day. Probably Pip Healy was the fifth.

got close enough to believe I saw pieces falling off this particular fellow before having to break away to avoid collision — the greatest danger in this kind of attack — and go straight down. And then when well clear I pulled out and climbed up again to have another go. This was what we were all supposed to be doing and was what Lambert and Vibert did; it wasn't what Campbell did and we never found out whether it was what Dobby did because he was shot down and killed.

It wasn't of course in Campbell's nature to stay with these kind of tactics and his story afterwards was approximately this:

'I got one on my first attack and was manoeuvering for another when I got hit. I went into a dive but when I tried to pull out the controls were dead and then when I tried to slide back the hood I couldn't — (probably a bullet or cannon shell had bent the runners) — By now I was moving too damn fast and if I didn't get out soon I never would so I undid my straps and butted the hood with my head and at the third butt I got out, hood and all. I was about to pull the rip cord when

I thought what the hell's the hurry and decided to look around. The first thing I saw was my machine falling past me and the next that my gun was falling beside me with the damn thing just out of reach. I tried like hell to edge over to it but I couldn't and anyway it speeded up pretty quickly and was way ahead of me. Then I remembered reading that in free flight there isn't much you can't do so I tried a few swallow dives and jack-knives and that was great. But I stopped it when I saw another kite going down and crash, pulled my cord and came down okay.'

I've never thought the story to be inaccurate — and the facts confirmed it. We never saw Harry Dobbyn again and Campbell, obviously lucky not to have broken his neck, was not to fly again. Most of us had stiff necks from constantly turning our heads to scan the sky — if you didn't do that you didn't last very long and Campbell couldn't turn his at all.

So, rather rapidly, we were down to four pilots and all sergeants. We discussed who should be what and decided to appoint Bertie Lambert commanding officer and me as acting commanding officer. I don't know if any other group of pilots ever had a sergeant commanding officer and in any case if we'd been accurate I suppose we ought to have titled ourselves flight commander and acting flight commander but it was a nice conceit and anyway we were to all intents and purposes a separate flying unit for the only time we saw the other half of the squadron was when one of us relieved the other. Vibert flew Number Two to Bertie and Pip Healey as Number Two to me. And that was that. We were to go on flying until by accident, strafing, casualties or unserviceableness the available aircraft were so reduced in numbers that the balance of 605s were given to 242 and in 'A' Flight at least there were to be no more casualties.

They became busy days. The telephone beside us rang unnervingly and ceaselessly — if you weren't smoking when it rang, the moment you knew it wasn't to tell you to scramble, you lit a cigarette. Probably you *were* smoking — we used to buy round tins of 50 Players and one didn't last a day. There was a system for that telephone: one ring was for us, two for the other squadron and three for both. One or two rings could be, and often were, for unimportant reasons; three rings meant scramble anyway.

We were on edge for the telephone ringing yet always startled when it did. We'd stop talking and our hearts would have begun to thud and we'd grip the chairs like mad. If there was no second ring Bertie would answer and maybe we'd be off or maybe not. If there was a second ring we'd relax, if only momentarily. On the third ring we'd pitch our cigarettes away and run like hell for the Hurricanes. The duty ground staff, warned by a ghastly hooter, would be alerted by the time we got to them — the mechanics already up into the cockpits, the others standing by the parachutes to help us into them. They were always left resting on the port mainplane with their straps dangling and what you did was to turn and offer your backs to them and as the shoulder straps were passed to you click their metal banded ends into slots in the quick release — which was a circular bit of metal about level with your navel — and grab the other two between your legs and click them home as well. Then, clumsy as a waddling duck, and puffed from running out and too much smoking you'd climb up into the cockpit.

The mechanics would have already started up the engines so that the aerodrome moments before quiet would be harsh with the snarl but quietening as you throttled back. The mechanics who had stepped from the cockpit on to the wing root to help you up would place the harness over your shoulders while you reached for the lower straps — this was a webbing harness each strap of which had a line of brass bound holes which fitted over a boss into which you slid a split pin so that a pilot could strap himself in as tightly as he chose but release himself instantly in emergency by drawing out the pin.

All this would be done in great haste as would be the fumbling with helmet, silk undergloves and gauntlets, the shoving of oxygen and R/T tubes dangling from one's helmet into appropriate sockets and the beginning of vital take off checks while already your instructions would be coming through.

'Scramble, Evitt aircraft! Scramble, Evitt aircraft! Priok Angels twenty five! Forty plus bandits approaching from the North West.'

We would wait for Bertie to start taxying out across the bumpy grass and follow him — Vibert, then me, then Healey. Our hoods would be open slid back in their runners, the bellow of the engines raucous in our ears, the smell of hot oil and petrol in our nostrils and our hearts fairly pounding in our chests. It was always the same — a hollowness in the stomach and a mingled sense of haste, excitement and trepidation.

Bertie would slew dangerously fast on to the runway, check his drift, slam his throttle open and be off with a tremendous full throated soon waning roar. After him would go Vibert. This was no take off in formation — this was getting into the air as quickly as you could. Vibert would be moving down the runway before Bertie was unstuck with us two following. With the aircraft not five feet off the ground Bertie's undercarriage would be going up and he'd be banking while he climbed towards the port of Tandjeonpriok and we would climb after him, Vibert tucking himself in just to his left and a little behind and I'd be a little farther away on his right with Pip Healey forming up on me. And we'd already be craning our stiff necks for a sight of Japanese in any quadrant of the sky.

The R/T would be jabbering at us:

'Evitt aircraft, Evitt aircraft — are you receiving me?'

You could see Bertie's hand move as he flicked the switch and hear his Middlesbrough voice:

'Okay, Rider, Evitt leader calling. Receiving you loud and clear. Red and Yellow Sections airborne. Are you receiving me?'

Back it would come:

'Evitt Leader, Evitt Leader, receiving you loud and clear. There are twenty seven bombers reported with about thirty fighters covering. Bombers at eighteen thousand feet.'

'Thank you for nothing, Rider', Bertie would say. 'Listening out.'

And Bertie would look at me and then at Vibert querying we'd heard and we'd thumb up at him we had.

We would be climbing hard at full throttle, only the cut out boost held back in reserve and the angle of flight would allow us only to see each other and the sky above. Our ears would be filled with the roar of engine sound and rushing slipstream and it would become cool, then cold, and at about twelve thousand feet we'd shut our hoods — and with them most of the noise outside. Now each of us was cocooned in a little perspex world, the bars of the hood, its framework, forming a pattern against the sky, the odd shaped, back sloping windscreen broken by the gunsight. Already we would have turned the brass milled wheel to 'Fire' — always a moment of drama when the roughness of the mill is felt even through layers of gloves.

At fifteen thousand feet we'd turn on oxygen. And all the time we'd be grinning at each other, the trepidation quite gone, sharing a unique experience, four young men three miles up, heading for seven miles up made one entity by the indescribable camaraderie of the empty sky.

We'd test our intercom:

'Hallo, Red Two, Red Leader calling. Are you receiving me? Over.'

'Hallo, Red Leader, Red Two calling. Receiving you loud and clear. Talk about SFA . . . '

We had our own codes now. Ten tenths cloud we called Pilot's Delight; no cloud at all was Sweet Fuck All. PD and SFA . . .

At twenty thousand we'd be more watchful still, turning our heads all the time — this way, that way, upwards, downwards, sideways . . . scanning the sky. The most important thing of all.

At thirty thousand it was the same but the formation more open now as our controls grew sloppier in the thinner air.

And the last few thousand feet would be a painful crawl with the knowledge that at thirty four thousand feet we'd be fireproof. Perhaps even at thirty two.

So far as we knew, apart from reconnaissance machines, there were no Japanese aircraft which could reach such a height. Certainly not a Navy Nought.

Yes, at thirty-four thousand feet you were fireproof — you could just cruise, watching and waiting, taking your time.

Manuals I have read more recently give maximum ceiling altitudes for the Navy 0 above thirty four thousand feet but I find this difficult to believe. One thing which was quite certain was that we never saw them at such heights and when they saw us above them at such heights the Navy 0 pilots never tried to come up to meet us. Perhaps they were carrying heavier fuel loads than the aircraft on which the data was based or the tropical air had some effect — we certainly worked on the assumption Hurricanes had superior ceilings and weren't to be disappointed.

When we saw the enemy it was always pretty much the same. The bombers at the lowest level, a screen of fighters above protecting them and a second screen higher still protecting the first. We didn't follow any set order of attack — we were really, I suppose, rather like four high level divers each with his own board deciding to make his dive when the fancy took him. I have no idea how much we achieved. Not a great deal obviously — you have to be lucky to score victories with these kind of tactics against an alert, manoeuverable enemy. The important thing was to be there at all, to maintain a fighter presence — if there was any purpose at all in flying in Java it was by being a nuisance to divert forces from elsewhere. So long as whenever the bombers arrived over Java there were fighters who might attack them, so long were the Japanese obliged to send quite large fighter screens in support. That we had some success is unquestionable because occasionally the wreck of a shot down Navy Nought would be reported — but whether or not it was 605 or 242s, 'A' Flight's or 'B' Flight's, Bertie's, Vibert's, Healey's or mine, no one can say. We didn't make claims. We'd have looked foolish in front of the others doing so — anyway there wasn't anyone to make claims to. Just the four of us sitting in that hut when we were flying and roaring round Batavia when we weren't.

One personal incident I had may explain both why there was so little time to judge the result of an attack and how it was that we managed to stay intact. It was a day of towering cumulus and our attack was made on a circle of Navy 0s orbiting within a chasm between two such cloud formations. I happened to be the first to peel off and having passed through the Japanese I steepened almost to the vertical, engine full bore, and looked back on the off chance of seeing if I'd had any luck. And I saw one of the most beautiful things I ever saw flying. Following me down were the other three and after them was peeling the whole formation of Navy Noughts. Every aircraft was sharp and clear against the background of white cumulus. It was like a film set but gigantic in scale, the actors miniscule but giving life to it — twenty, thirty aircraft all in a screaming vertical power dive against a pure white background with the green and red of the land hurtling upwards and the blue above. It was quite unforgettable.

I watched it far too long. By the time I looked away I must have dived vertically at full throttle for seven or eight thousand feet and when I tried to start easing out, I found there was nothing I could do. The controls were frozen solid.

I throttled back and putting my other hand on the control column heaved on it with all my strength thrusting with my feet and it was to absolutely no effect. I was travelling too fast and the control were locked. There wasn't time to feel afraid, there never is in such circumstances and you don't get blood leaking from the corner of your mouth or any of that nonsense the film makers are so keen on. You just understand very clearly the predicament you're in and that if you don't find a way out of it quickly you will soon be dead. The whole of your past life doesn't flash in front of you and you don't have visions of that dreadful moment of impact — you're much too busy.

It was obvious that baling out wasn't any good — at the sort of speed I'd by now reached, probably terminal velocity, if I'd even managed to get my head out of the cockpit it would have been torn off and even if it wasn't the tail fin would probably just about slice me in two. So that wasn't on. And if I couldn't do anything with the stick there was only one thing left — the tail trim.

In a Hurricane there were minute strips of metal like tiny elevators on the trailing edges of the elevators themselves which were adjustable by turning a relatively large wheel inside the cockpit. Like the smallest weights on a balance, these strips could be moved fractionally to give perfect fore and aft balance so that in normal flight the stick is absolutely neutral — indeed that is their purpose. One was always instructed to treat tail trim with great respect and it was often said that misuse at high speeds could tear off the tailplane. Now to use it was Hobson's choice.

I took one hand off the stick and wound the trim wheel the merest fraction towards myself and at once grabbing at the stick again hauled on it with all my strength. And I was rewarded by the faintest softness, the slightest yielding. Hanging on like grim death with one hand, thrusting with my feet, my back pressed hard against the shield of armour plate behind me, I clung to my gain and wound the trim the merest fraction more and again grabbed at the stick and heaved. And I knew I was going to be all right — that I had left the vertical. I still had to be very careful — too much exuberance would pull the Hurricane apart. But I was winning. The G in my head was intense and the aircraft, normally so light felt like a lorry load of lead and I could almost feel the huge strain on the wings myself. But I was winning. I began to see the red and green world below which had been fixed begin to slide away behind me as the nose came up, all the time accelerating until at length there was the horizon and I was flying straight and level.

I reversed the trim, busy talking to myself as I found I always did under these kind of circumstances. I looked at the altimeter — fifteen thousand feet. Quite a long dive. I looked at the airspeed indicator and couldn't believe my eyes. Three hundred odd miles an hour! And the first thing that crossed my mind was that if that was all that I was doing I'd soon have that shower of Navy 0s on my tail. Anyway how could I be only doing three hundred odd miles an hour after what must have been a dive of terminal velocity. Glaring at the altimeter, I saw that the speed was dropping fast — as it should, I told myself, aloud, throttled right back as I was. And it was then, of course, that the penny dropped. I'd gone right round the clock not once, but twice! I watched it absolutely fascinated, seeing it complete a counter revolution, pass through the four hundred miles an hour at one o'clock on the inner scale and then through two hundred and forty miles an hour at five o'clock on the outer one. It should, I thought, be all right now. I pushed the throttle open experimentally and after a moment or two the airspeed began to pick up again.

There is a rule of thumb for converting true flying speed from the speed indicated by the instruments which, working on air pressure, underwrite your speed the higher you climb. You add for every thousand feet of height one and three quarter per cent to the indicated speed. Even by the time I was flying straight and level I had been flying at more than five hundred and ninety miles an hour. The vertical speed must have been knocking the speed of sound.

It is a remarkable achievement for the designer of an aircraft with a top straight and level speed of about three hundred and thirty miles an hour that it could be put to such a test and emerge triumphant; it seemed that much more remarkable when compared with the disintegration of its rival at Palembang.

There was no doubt about it, I thought, as I flew along, looking affectionately at the sturdy wings with their rows of rivets — as Arthur Sheerin had once said to me: 'She's a sweet, bloody marvellous, wonderful kite.'

★ ★ ★

I don't remember all that clearly those last few days of flying apart from incidents such as the above. We got strafed and bombed once or twice; I remember being in a slit trench with an Air Vice Marshal and a cannon shell lodging in the wall above his head missing it by a few inches and how he wanted to fly one of our Hurricanes for old times' sake and we gave him permission on the agreement that if there was a flap he'd fly two to Bertie. (What a line! 'I remember when I had an Air Vice Marshal as my Number Two.') I remember Pip Healey roaring across the airfield at nought feet chasing a Navy 0. I remember we got interviewed by someone or other who was making a broadcast home; he gave us a slap up dinner at the Hotel des Indes in the Mowlenviet and I think that perhaps after all it was he who had the yacht at Tandjeonpriok, not our host with the open cellar — he took a note of our names and where we lived. I don't suppose he made the broadcast. The sands were running out too fast. I remember getting very drunk, all of us getting very drunk, hiring four bicycle rickshaws and putting the drivers in the passenger seats and having a furious race round Batavia; I remember Julie.

And I remember the last day we flew. March 1st 1942.

★ ★ ★

An hour before dawn the telephone awakened us at our house ordering us to Tjillitan. We snatched a last cup of coffee and drove to the airfield in the Bedford and were there informed that the Japanese had landed on Java at three points: one directly opposite the Sunda Straits where they had apparently penetrated no less than 60 kilometres before being reported, another near Cheribon some sixty miles or so east of Batavia where they were still landing, and a third near Soerabaya about four hundred miles further east.

We were ordered to attack the landings at Cheribon, 242 Squadron having already done so and lost one pilot in the process.

We made three flights, one a particularly memorable one.

This was the second sortie and there were five Hurricanes flown by Wright, a Sergeant Young of 242 Squadron, Bertie, Pip and me. We flew, I remember, overland in an open 'V' finding the sky clear of cloud apart from a mass of cumulus near the coast. Approaching the landing zone we were diverted by the sight of a single Japanese seaplane presumably on patrol to protect from submarines the invasion fleet — (although to give it such a name was to say the very least a slight exaggeration).

We fell into line astern with Wright commencing the attack while I was ruefully reflecting that it was just my luck to be fifth in line with such a sitting target. I was mistaken. The Japanese pilot proved himself resourceful, capable and daring. He immediately dropped his bomb load or depth charges which exploded in the clear shallow sea creating a fascinating coral atoll pattern and instead of making for the cloud or diving for the sea either of which manoeuvres would have been suicidal, maintained his height, banked astonishingly steeply and with our engines throttled right back to give the maximum time for the supposed en route destruction of this cumbersome machine was suddenly not the pursued but the pursuer. Round and round the six of us went in a mad tight circle with the gunner in the seaplane blazing away at me and as I broke, Pip Healey and so on, forcing each in turn to take evasive action.

Now we were thoroughly disorganised and more than that from a personal point of view I appeared to have sprung some minor oil leak because my windscreen partially clouded over. On reflection I suppose the proper thing for Wright to have done was to have detailed a couple of Hurricanes to deal with the seaplane leaving the rest of us to carry on to the landing zone. Perhaps radio communication had broken down again — I don't know. I just know that there were no instructions and it became a free for all.

I saw Wright, an experienced pilot with twelve victories to his credit and the Distinguished Flying Medal attack and fail. I saw Bertie attack and fail.

I turned away to give myself distance and came in for my own attack and the seaplane, grey camouflaged, all but disappeared against the dirty windscreen. I had to bank for fear of ramming it and as I did so another Hurricane came whistling past me far too close for comfort.

And so it went on. What ought to have been a disciplined attack became a shambles with Hurricanes more likely to shoot each other down or collide than be successful. The problem was the astonishing manoeuverability of the seaplane which seemed to have the ability to turn as tightly as a Tiger Moth. It was here, there and everywhere with five fighters buzzing round it, coming in on a random attack only to break away as they saw another coming in to attack as well. Not that this is new — there have been many occasions where markedly less manoeuverable aircraft have escaped it, similar circumstances.

After a while, there was unspoken agreement to hold back and let Wright take the fellow on alone. We watched, frustrated. He made attack after attack but the will o' the wisp avoided each one until finally out of ammunition, he set off back to Tjillitan to rearm with Bertie and Pip following him. It was better now there were just the two of us and no danger really of collision — we both attacked singly and in the end Young shot it down.

With plenty of petrol and ammunition left I couldn't see any reason for going back to Tjillitan so set off for the invasion zone. The 'fleet' consisted of a mere four transports and three destroyers and troops were coming ashore in all manner of small craft from sampans upwards and none very large. They were difficult to attack effectively and it was all rather different from on the Moesi. There almost every bullet counted — here the vast majority sprayed an empty sea. Still there were a lot of targets and one could on a run manage more than one at a time. There were targets ashore as well — an established gun emplacement which gave its position away by firing at me and being right out in the open, surprisingly, was unprotected and easily silenced and a couple more seaplanes rather cleverly drawn up in small palm girt coves of which I managed to set one on fire and whose destruction was confirmed later in prison camp.

It was an altogether exciting and memorable few minutes with no Navy 0s about and the only opposition the flak from the destroyers — they managed to get my height but not my range (it's very difficult to hit a low flying aircraft travelling at several hundred miles an hour) and I could see the shrapnel kicking up small puffs of sand below me and the shells bursting nearby and looking exactly like sea urchins.

But the picture I remember most clearly, in fact I'm not at all sure it isn't out of the whole war the picture I remember best of all, is of the first Japanese I saw really close to. I only saw him for a split second but the image is fixed like an image on a film by the click of a camera shutter; he was wearing dark green shorts and a yellow shirt. He had no cap on and he was kneeling in the surf on an unprotected sandy beach looking over his shoulder at me as I came inland at about twenty feet after a strafing run . . . and he looked absolutely terrified.

Of the flying part of 258 experiences there is little more to say — and nothing which wouldn't be repetition. We refuelled and rearmed and made one more sortie and then on landing handed our machines over to the other Flight which had come to relieve and went off, thankfully, for lunch in Batavia.

266

Although we didn't know it we had made our last wartime flights.

★ ★ ★

In this account I have not attempted to catalogue results and have only mentioned those which were part of incidents such as that of the seaplane on March 1st in which the story would have been incomplete without such mention.

I couldn't give more than an incomplete list of victories known and claimed and to include these would be invidious to other pilots. In fact I should very much doubt there were any 258 pilots who flew long enough who didn't have their share of certain victories, their probables and their possibles and few who weren't involved in the Moesi strafing, in strafing in Singapore or in strafing on the Java landings. I think it fair to leave it like that.

Of the 22 pilots who had left Abbotsinch, by the time Java fell five had been confirmed killed and one was missing, one was interned (to escape and be killed later), two were injured (both to be killed later), five were prisoners and only eight (of which three were to be killed later) were still available for flying.

It is fair to ask whether these losses were worthwhile and I suppose the answer varies according to points of view. We certainly did kill a lot of Japanese and we shot down a fair number of their aircraft — on the other hand it is doubtful if we held up the invasions of Sumatra and Java, or their capitulations by as much as a single day.

It could well have been another story — if only Micky Maguire had had his way.

11

Slowly into the Bag

WE lunched well and went back to our house to a message from Victor de la Perelle, one of the squadron pilots who having been put in charge of administration had scarcely flown. A likeable man, Perelle, with a face badly scarred from a German cannon shell which had disintegrated inside his cockpit when he was shooting up a flakship in June of 1941 — and a sad man too: Roy Keedwell had become his closest friend.

The message was that the four remaining Hurricanes of 605 were to be handed over to 242 and all other pilots would be leaving for the southern port of Tjiliatjap for embarkation following the other 258 pilots who had already left from the same port a few hours earlier.

The decision had followed a letter written four days earlier by Air

Commodore Vincent to the Air Officer Commanding West Group:

'RAF Base Headquarters
Batavia.
February 25th 1942

'We are getting very short of Fighter Defence in this forward sector. This afternoon we are actually down to 6 serviceable aircraft between the two Squadrons.

'All being well, we shall get back to a total of 10 or 11 tomorrow. We are not likely ever to better that figure owing to daily casualties, and the force is definitely wasting.

'The Dutch are, I am told, not using the Hurricanes that we gave them operationally, and they have also removed all their Fighters from Tjisaoek so that our meagre force is all there is in the front line.

'Is it possible for us to get the Hurricanes back, or at least persuade the Dutch to bring them perhaps to Semplak or Tjisaoek to share out some of the very strenuous flying and fighting that our Squadrons are doing?

'If we cannot get any more aircraft I think the time has come to shrink to one Squadron, and I would suggest, if this is done, that 605 should go ('though the airmen are quite among the very best as workers and "fighters") and 242 should stay, as they have more pilots. They should take on the few pilots from 605 also.

'At the moment Tjisaoek is our reserve aerodrome. I am moving the R & R party from Tjiloungair tomorrow morning as it is so very much better. I went yesterday to Tjisaoek to ask the Dutch Commandant to carry out any R & R work necessary but found the Dutch had flown. We have no other reserve aerodrome except Tjisomang which is near Bandoeng and I have not been able to visit that. My Dutch Liaison Officer whom I asked to get particulars, measurements, communications etc., has absconded (with a personal debt of twenty guilders to me) so I am not in the picture I am afraid there.

'I want to go into the question of an alternative Operations Room further back in case our present one is 'blitzed' perhaps in Buitenzorg or even Bandoeng. I would like to have your views on this first, however, on the advisability of the labour, wiring, equipment etc. With regard to our few RDF sets do you think we could put one at Tjilatjap where it could at least give warnings — though probably not much more.

'I have now spoken to you on the telephone on the first part of this letter but I would like it on paper also,

'Yours,

(Vincent)

Second thoughts were to carry the day and were, unfortunately too late, to consider it wiser to send the by now experienced 605 pilots to a new theatre of operations rather than add them to a squadron which already had far more than enough pilots for its few machines. The 226 Group records read:

'On the 27th (February) Air Vice Marshal Maltby AOC MOURAIR (so renamed from West Group) visited Batavia. He was very favourably impressed by the efficiency of the operations room and the excellent morale and spirit of the fighter pilots and ground personnel and instructed Air Commodore Vincent to leave the country next day together with as many of his staff as possible. He thought that the group might reform in Ceylon. Air Vice Marshal Maltby had stated on 22.2.42 that on 3.3.42 a decision would be taken regarding Fighter Aircraft reinforcement of Java or elsewhere.

'On the afternoon of the 28th Air Commodore Vincent with seven members of his staff proceeded to Bandeong where they were instructed by Air Vice Marshal Maltby to carry on through the night to Tjilatjap where they boarded the SS *Zaandam* which was alleged to be proceeding to Colombo. The ship was diverted to Fremantle where it arrived on 6th March.

'The two squadrons were left in the charge of Wing Commander Maguire but owing to wastage one squadron only — Number 242 — was operated and the pilots of 605 Squadron under Squadron Leader Wright, were sent off to evacuate if possible. It is hoped that these personnel may be in Ceylon or India, if not they are presumed to be prisoners of war.'

We left, in fact, late on the afternoon of March 1st in our Bedford van with Bertie Lambert driving. After all but falling into Japanese hands by taking a wrong turning we caught up with a large convoy heading south towards Bandoeng. There was much rumour and little real information and the rest of us sat in the back with rifles and Tommy Guns we had managed to lay our hands on at the ready. But the road was hilly and tortuous and lorries ahead of us in the convoy continually broke down obliging us to pick up stragglers and we were soon so packed out we could hardly in an emergency have used these arms.

All in all it was a dramatic enough night with the thought of escape sharpening apprehension of the possibility of ambush and with the thrill and novelty of the first night any of us had known journeying through a beautiful tropical land. The roads were packed, not simply by our convoy moving southwards but by

Dutch and Indonesian troops heading northwards begging for information which no one could give. There was no sense of panic but there was huge confusion and uncertainty.

We arrived at Bandoeng at eight in the morning of March 2nd expecting to refuel and pass straight through to Tjilatjap. Had we done so we would have avoided being taken prisoner. But it was not to be — for no reason which made any sense to us, or which was ever discovered, we were ordered to remain and two precious days slipped by in idleness while news, or at any rate rumour, grew more and more disquieting. Shipping at Tjilatjap was, we were told, being heavily attacked and most ships leaving port were promptly sunk by Japanese submarines. It was probably nonsense. What was not nonsense were the daily formations of Japanese bombers attacking the nearby airfield of Andir to which 242 had withdrawn with the last remaining Hurricanes.

We were quartered in the military barracks of Tymahi, fretting with impatience as each passing hour diminished the possibility of escape on, for example, longer range aircraft quitting Andir for Australia. We lived in great style but this was the only consolation and the town was permeated with the same depressing atmosphere of defeatism we had first experienced at P2 on the way up to Singapore. Everywhere the Japanese advanced and almost so it seemed, unresisted; there were no suggestions as to how they might be halted, nor knowledge of any opposing them.

It seemed absurd. Through strafing one of the invading forces, through in fact being of the very few of the military milling round ever to have fired a shot in anger, we felt entitled to be angry.

Although we were only two days in Bandoeng with each hour so precious it seemed many more. On March 4th belated instructions were given that all pilots must be evacuated and we were supplied with two Ford V-8s with orders that at all costs Tjilatjap must be made by midnight or the ship we were to board would have already sailed. We left at dusk — our iron rations, crates of champagne and bully beef. There

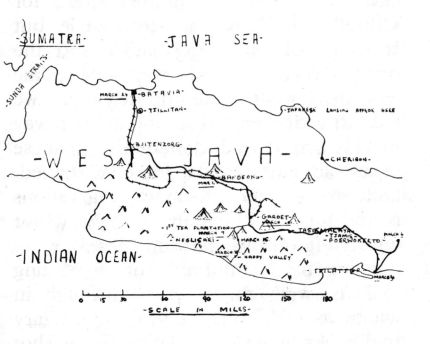

Map drawn by the author in prison camp showing attempted escape route.

were ten of us: in one car Campbell, de la Perelle, Lambert, Healey and myself Wright, Vibert and three others in the second.

That drive was thrilling and quite unforgettable. The night was glorious, as bright as day, tile road all but deserted, the route through fantastic scenery — hills and valleys, forests,

277

jungle, rice-fields; and rivers and lakes silver in the brilliant moonlight. Swarms of fireflies lit our way and the jungles were shrieking with tree frogs and cicadas. As on the road to Bandoeng we lost our way, driving for perhaps twenty miles in a false direction and were stopped at a road block manned by Indonesians a mile, we were told, from the Japanese. We turned and drove more furiously than ever, taking turn and turn about at the wheel, consulting our watches, doing arithmetic, opening bottle on bottle of champagne and throwing the empties through the windows. We shrieked through dark and silent kampongs, talked incessantly, bellowed 'Aloha' at the night. We knew that midnight wasn't possible — Tjilatjap was too far. But we didn't believe we would be taken prisoner, we were too young and optimistic — we didn't believe fate would cheat us at the very end. If necessary we told ourselves the boat would wait . . . anyway when did a boat ever sail to time?

★ ★ ★

It was two o'clock when we arrived on the outskirts of the town which was forebodingly still and, apart from the insect sounds, quite silent. We had no idea of the direction of the docks and there was no one about to tell us. We could see no signs and the moon had set. We paused, one car, the other left behind, and were deep in a council of war when we saw an armed man approaching. He was Oriental and, we assumed Indonesian. As best we could with barely a word of Malay between us we asked him to direct us to the docks. He did so — and at once melted into the blackness. We took the road suggested and with every yard it grew gloomier and gloomier, the trees closing in, narrowing to a dusty cart track at its end. With each passing moment imagination took strength and we began to ask ourselves and then each other if our guide hadn't been Javanese but Japanese. We stopped the cars, dismounted, revolvers in our hands, prepared for ambush.

But there was nothing, no ambush and no docks. Just the empty silent threatening night. We were fevered by impatience and frustration, imagining even at that moment our ship weighing anchor, leaving us behind. And then another man approached. He was a Dutch officer. He was quite to the point. There were no ships. The last ship had been sunk by dive bombers the previous day. It wouldn't have made any difference even if we had arrived by midnight.

I suppose that was something of a consolation, but not a very great one. We were deflated; it was a dreadful anti-climax. And although we wouldn't admit to it, we realised the last hope had gone — there on a hot tropical night in a dusty, gloomy lane in a tawdry little dockyard town on the South coast of Java.

We found a hotel, its owner bemused by circumstances, his last guest gone. He shrugged his shoulders and left us to our own devices. We drank his champagne, used his kitchen and slept fitfully in armchairs in the lounge. There were, presumably, ample beds available — we never thought of using them.

In the morning we were bombed. The

hotel was located in the centre of a complex of gun emplacements. The first bombing was by heavy bombers which made their run directly over us. When they had finished we went outside. At once we heard the sound of approaching aircraft — but these weren't heavy bombers. Bertie looked up. 'Hurricanes!' he shouted. 'Five in a Vic and one in the box!' But then we saw the bombs begin to fall. We threw ourselves to the ground and after the bombs had exploded ran back into the hotel and for want of a better place dived under the billiard table. There were succeeding waves and the hotel was struck. The noise was appalling and to a pattern: the hum of approaching engines, the increasing roar as the dive bombers came in for their attack, the by now familiar 'cudumph, cudumph, cudumph' of Bofors guns, machine gun fire, the whistling of bombs, the thud of explosions all around and very near, the waning sound of aircraft overtaken by a new formation beginning it all again.

Soon all around us was a welter of debris. The windows were all blown in and glass was everywhere, part of the roof collapsed burying the billiard table with bricks, laths, tiles and plaster and everywhere was thick dust. Just across the road a house was blazing. It seemed obvious the hotel was a death trap. In a lull between one raid and the next we raced for the cover of a ditch across the road. All around were fires and from the nearby railway yard ammunition trains were burning and exploding with the most tremendous concussion. Dead were lying in the street. As the next formation began its dive we raced across the road and flung ourselves into the ditch, a drain in fact and in it crouching low was Wright. As we got our heads down we heard the guns begin to fire and the whistling of bombs.

It lasted for about an hour — a very personal attack. When it was over we went back into the hotel which had, after all, miraculously escaped complete destruction. But the lounge was an awesome sight. And here and there where we had put them down were glasses of champagne — and each wore a thick white layer of plaster dust — like cream.

We spent that day and night at Tjilatjap, trying to formulate a plan. We knew nothing of the country, we had no Malay, we could obtain no reliable information. The town lay under a pall of smoke from a writhing cauliflower reddened by internal flames which was all that remained of an ammunition dump. We watched with envious eyes a Catalina flying boat daring to reconnoitre and discussed crackpot schemes of inching our way by sampan along all the islands, Java, Bali, Sumba, Sumbawa, Timor, to Darwin. We drank champagne and smoked endless cigarettes.

There was no point in staying at Tjilatjap and after that gruelling morning of March 5th, the Japanese didn't bother to bomb it — there was nothing left worthwhile to bomb. On the morning of the sixth we set off in the direction of Jogyakarta where, we had been told we might catch a boat — by the time we arrived at Purworego we realised that Jogyakarta was inland. As we drove into Purworego the troops in it were moving out advising us the Japanese were expected imminently — although where they could have come from I can't imagine. We provisioned and turned eastwards.

There were only two possibilities unless we tried the sampan venture, which reflection told us that without knowledge of seamanship would have been slow suicide even if we found the sampan which was hardly likely — to take to the bush or be taken prisoner. Taking to the bush would have been much like taking to a sampan except that even had we managed to survive it would have been only a matter of time before the Javanese betrayed us to the Japanese — as indeed they did a small group by then ridden with amoebic dysentery who joined us subsequently in our prison camp. And if we were to be taken prisoner the wise thing was as part of a large group, not a small band to be summarily slaughtered because of their nuisance value.

So we drove eastwards not back through Tjilatjap but inland, picking up the Bandoeng road again and spending the night at a small town named Tjamis, sleeping on straw paliasses in a barn, washing in rank well water, eating native food.

Chaos was everywhere. There were convoys passing in opposite directions, each with its own differing information, its own barely formulated plans. Japanese aircraft were continually overhead, strafing the roads, bombing nearby objectives. Rumour was rife, rumour and counter rumour; and despair was as intermingled with hope. There was no way of halting the Japanese — yet it was impossible to conceive that such a vast country with its teeming millions could be overrun by such a small number of enemy. A stand would be made somewhere.

On the seventh we drove on eastwards, camouflaging the V-8s with banana tree fronds at every halt, diving into muddy ditches when the road was strafed. At Tasikmalaya we met our Defence Office Pilot Officer Taute going the other way; we didn't discuss the Japanese raid on P1 with paratroops — P1 was nearly six hundred miles away and a thousand years in time. But we talked about something else. He told us that 232 Squadron had flown until their last Hurricane had been destroyed and then two Lockheed

Loadstars were detailed to fly them to Australia. Their Commanding Officer, a Squadron Leader Brooker and several other pilots had already left in the first and the rest were in the second, about to leave, when they were ordered out by a Dutch Officer and his entourage at the point of Tommy guns. The Dutch went instead. Was it truth or fable? It could have been true — with our experience of the Dutch in Java we believed it was.

The next day was March 8th. Still heading eastwards we were overtaken by a contingent of native troops in a truck from which fluttered a huge Japanese flag. The troops did not seem in the least depressed. It was, they told, us, all over. Java had capitulated. After eight days the most modest force of Japanese had, practically without opposition, invested the enormous island and secured its vast resources. Now the decision, toyed with previously, had to be made. Did we take to the jungle, untrained, without radio equipment, without the language, in a country whose natives were already sensing liberation from their Dutch masters armed only with revolvers and a few rounds of ammunition — or did we accept what the men in the endless convoys passing and repassing had accepted? That it was over. That it was up to other men.

We finally decided against the jungle and the squadron documents were destroyed; we were still not quite without hope some miracle would happen. It was possible that all the bad news was rumour — no one we met, or indeed were to meet in the next two weeks, had met or would in that time see, except in the air, a single Japanese. That was quite remarkable — for the next two weeks thousand upon thousand of British troops, admittedly mostly non-combatant: air force groundstaff, army ordinance, cooks, pay clerks, signallers — the tail of military units, largely unarmed, devoid of a real leader, would wander without the least let or hindrance through vast tracts of Java while their conquerors must have wondered who were these men who had ruled the largest Empire the world had ever known.

We overtook a major convoy and fell in with it and heading south spent the night encamped at a large tea plantation known as Neglisari, a delightful spot high up in the hills from which a tantalising triangle of sea could just be seen. Our quarters were a tanning shed, our ablutions done in an ice cold mountain stream.

In the morning we were addressed by Air Vice Marshal Maltby to the effect our fighting days were over. We rebelled and leaving the huge convoy headed further south towards the sea, spending the night sleeping as best we could in the V-8s. The next morning we came on the ground staff of 605 Squadron. They had searched the coast a mere ten or fifteen miles distant. There were no boats — except for the hills there was nowhere to go. The empty sea lay to the south and to the north, at Garoet, were the Japanese — a vital town where there was a railway terminus and which lay on the road from Bandoeng to Tjilatjap and the whole of Southern Java.

We conferred — and decided to throw in our lot with 605.

We dubbed our new camp 'Happy Valley' and it was indeed as near to Shangri-La as anything imaginable. There were high hills all around and a torrential river conveniently broadened itself into a deep safe swimming pool. It was often wet but always warm; the scenery was superb. The rich land of Java yielded ample supplies — eggs, chicken, fruit and vegetables to relieve the monotony of tinned supplies. We tried buffalo and found it sweet but palatable, we chewed brown bars of molasses shaped like seaside rock.

Quite soon a sense of peace fell over Happy Valley, illogical but mesmerising, bringing with it feelings of permanence. Native huts, vermin ridden, papered with old newspapers, were commandeered and cleaned and we began to talk of planting vegetables and studying for examinations. No aircraft bothered us — there could well have been no enemy nearer than Japan itself. Out of initial chaos, discipline began to reassert itself and rank to count. The beginnings of a structure formed, daily routine orders were issued and fatigues arranged. Suddenly there was no war any more — merely a large group of Britishers who had taken possession of a corner of a foreign land and were settling into it as in a province.

This lasted for a week when orders were received from the Dutch Command to move northwards, past Neglisari, to another tea plantation at Palempoek. The roads looked different now being littered with the accoutrements of a defeated army which had destroyed all it could — wrecked cars, lorries lying smashed in ditches, spiked Bofors guns and burnt out Bren gun carriers were everywhere — it seemed astonishing with so much equipment to destroy it hadn't been possible to hold the Japanese. The scenery was magnificent with the road, rarely level, winding its way through mountain sides and into valleys paddy field and jungle.

The plantation at Palempoek was the biggest yet and the best equipped. There was a football pitch, tennis courts, a swimming pool. Again we settled in — again the sense of permanence developed. There were new huts to rid of spiders, lizards, fleas and rats with more newspapers brittle and brown with age to strip from the walls. More chicken, buffalo steaks, and gula — as the molasses was called — to buy; more vegetables to plant. An attitude, astounding now to contemplate, that the Japanese would leave the camp to its own devices providing they were not provoked, took hold. Day followed day, leisurely and pleasant with nothing to do but laze, swim, talk, smoke, eat and watch football matches played against the local Javanese. Perhaps it was as well — after the jagged weeks we needed rest for what was to lie ahead.

Then came the first instructions from the conquerors — their prisoners were to march to Batavia, some two hundred miles away and be there in six days. The Japanese would, they said, take care of stragglers.

Then these instructions were countermanded and new ones issued — the prisoners, using their own transport, would move north to Garoet.

I never discovered how it came about that I should accompany a much tattooed first world war veteran, Squadron Leader Wigram to act as advance liaison with the Japanese. We drove, just the two of us, in a private car on March 20th and were quite unmolested meeting the first Japanese on the outskirts of the town. Apart from the one who had looked up at me from the beach at Cheribon, this was the first I had seen at close quarters. He was sentry on guard duty and he had his back very definitely to a wall and his rifle gripped very firmly indeed and his eyes were flickering in every direction as if he suspected that at any moment someone might shoot him.

It was altogether a very curious business and we had the sense that the Japanese arranging with us where their new batch of prisoners were to be billetted, having first to ascertain how many they would be, were equally nonplussed by the situation. The prisoners already in the town outnumbered their captors several times and had taken over much of its administration with Military Police on point duty controlling traffic, and others, like ourselves, commandeering accommodation, organising food supplies or simply wandering round shopping and sightseeing. The few Japanese who held Garoet on the other hand were mystified and ill at ease and they looked very small and puny in comparison with their captives, and their uniforms oddly comical.

It was hard to take them seriously.

Later in the day the main force of prisoners drove in in a convoy which for all the Japanese knew could well have been bristling with hidden arms, increasing the disproportion of captured to captor. One had the sense that it only needed someone to suggest the town should be taken from the Japanese and it could have been accomplished in short order.

Yet when absurdity seemed to have been stretched to breaking point, this was to be shown to be far from so for the Japanese puzzled as to some means by which their captives should occupy their time either suggested or accepted the suggestion of daily route marches out into the country. And over the next three days there was the remarkable spectacle of large bodies of prisoners stepping it out three abreast, singing their dirty marching songs, quite unaccompanied by guards, leaving their captors miles behind but dutifully returning to them in time for tea.

I found it difficult to rid myself of the feeling that some extraordinary mistake had happened. These Japanese . . . Where were the brutes who had, they said, manacled men's wrists with rusty nuts and bolts, shot helpless men to death in the ditches of Sumatra, used prisoners for bayonet practice? Not these men, surely? Not these nervous, shabby little dwarfs who stood blinking at us myopically as we marched by them lustily singing our bawdy songs and keeping splendid step . . . 'Left, right, left, right, left right left. Right whee . . . el! Oh the eagles they fly high, in Mobile. Oh the eagles they fly high, in Mobile. Oh the eagles they fly high, and they shit right in your eye, it's a good thing cows don't fly, in Mobile . . . Left, right, left, right, left right left . . . '

I was haunted by the same curious feeling which must have overtaken the troops meeting in No Man's Land on that first Christmas Day of 1914. That this could only be . . . a mistake. Because where was the animosity? The threat? Perhaps, I wondered, the British and the Japanese had secretly made it up. Perhaps there were negotiations going on and orders had been given out to those in the know on either side to keep a low profile until the 't's' had been crossed and the 'i's' dotted. That would have made sense of it — as far as I could see the only thing that would.

But the dream came to its appointed end. On the night of March 23rd we were instructed to march to a railway station some miles away. It was a cool night with the way lighted by small encampments of British Army units by the roadside. It was not unpleasant, marching along in the magic of the night, singing. Better than on the daily marches in the awful heat. And probably a worthwhile thing to do because it would be better back in Batavia with its facilities; worth the long and, by the end, rather weary drag.

The train pulled out at 6 a.m. There was plenty of room and the Japanese presented each prisoner with two packets of cigarettes and the run was fascinating. In the late afternoon we drew into the outskirts of Batavia and Dutch girls lined the track and waved to us as if we were the conquerors rather than the conquered.

It happened that as we pulled into the station I was standing behind Squadron Leader Wigram. He was obviously determined to put a good face on things, to show he didn't give a fig for the Japanese, that he at least didn't intent to truckle to them. He deliberately sat on the carriage step so that his legs were dangling casually as we pulled in.

Illusions abruptly died. A Japanese officer his face suffused with rage ran up and as the train came to a stop was savagely beating the old man about his legs with his cane and slapping him about the face . . .

We were marched through the streets with indecent haste like cows being herded off to market; there would have been a dignity in it if we'd been allowed to march in step.

We turned a corner and came in

sight of a sombre shabby looking set of buildings approached by an unmade dusty road and girt by high limewhited walls with higher roofed corner turrets from which armed Japanese stared down at us. The red ball on white of the Nippon flag fluttered mockingly.

'God!' I heard someone shout 'It's a bloody prison!'

There was a crude and shabby portico of concrete leading to a set of iron doors with barred openings above. The two centre doors were open. We were bundled through, past a tallyman. Every sixth prisoner was booted and at each booting the tallyman made a mark.

Inside was a large open courtyard made by an inner wall which the turrets straddled and directly ahead of us a huge cage with sides made of bars which men were clutching.

We passed the cage and doors were opened on a line of cells and a hundred and fifty were counted off and allocated, crowded into a fearful room with a concrete floor and tiny barred windows high up in the walls. Heavy doors were slammed, locked and barred upon us. We had arrived — in the native gaol of Boei Glodok.

But at least we were still together, Bertie Lambert, Pip Healey and myself — the last three pilots of the old 258 to fly.

Epilogue

IT would be foolhardy to claim there are no inaccuracies in this account — thirty five years is a long time and memory fades. There were a few notes, photographs and a log book I managed to keep hidden from the Japanese through many searches and I have, by studying official records, managed to remove a number of crashing blunders from an original draft. But, excepting the quotations from these records, on the whole what is contained in these pages is drawn from personal recollection and must, by necessity, have errors.

I make no apology on account of this for this is no attempt to write an official history but merely to tell the story of a short but exciting period in the life of a fighter squadron as seen largely through the eyes of one of its junior pilots. For the same reasons I have made no attempt to bring the contents linguistically up to date. I have called a Navy 0, a Navy 0 (and sometimes a Navy Nought) because they were not called Zekes or Zeros then, and I have spelt the names of towns as I would have spelt them at the time. I have expressed views which may well not have stood up to the test of history but these were the views I and my friends held at the time and what happened to these men and what they felt is what these pages are all about.

There is no claim made, nor intended, that 258 Squadron shone in bravery, ability or success, nor that it had a lion's share of the action; on the contrary 232 Squadron would have had a longer and certainly more successful tale to tell, while other squadrons such as 488 played at least equal parts. But it is of 258, I write.

Where, however, I must apologise, is for any errors, exaggerations, oversights or the like which cause pain; if I have transposed the actions of two pilots, I apologise; if I have improperly slighted by omission, I apologise; if I have unjustifiably indicated any lack of courage or resolution to any individual or groups of men, I apologise. But, saving these possibilities, all that I have written is so far as I have been able to set it down as accurate as memory supported only by the research indicated above allows. Only recently I read a first class account of naval operations in this theatre of war; there was an immense bibliography, no less than eighty-seven books were noted in it. The author was entitled to be believed. For a while I was tempted but in the end I ran away from it; my heart quailed at the thought of the books I would have to read, the libraries I would have to visit, the letters throughout the world I would have to write.

But there was an even more important consideration. Of the 258 Squadron pilots who left Abbotsinch on that bleak November morning in 1941 about half survived the war. I could before I set about this book have been in touch with every one of them and if any of them chance upon it, they may perhaps wonder why I did not. The answer is that memories which I have carried for so long have become old friends and if I had upset them now they would have been very doubtful allies in an attempt to set down something as it seemed to be, thirty five years back in time.

Other titles in the
Ulverscroft Large Print Series:

TO FIGHT THE WILD
Rod Ansell and Rachel Percy

Lost in uncharted Australian bush, Rod Ansell survived by hunting and trapping wild animals, improvising shelter and using all the bushman's skills he knew.

COROMANDEL
Pat Barr

India in the 1830s is a hot, uncomfortable place, where the East India Company still rules. Amelia and her new husband find themselves caught up in the animosities which seethe between the old order and the new.

THE SMALL PARTY
Lillian Beckwith

A frightening journey to safety begins for Ruth and her small party as their island is caught up in the dangers of armed insurrection.

FATAL RING OF LIGHT
Helen Eastwood

Katy's brother was supposed to have died in 1897 but a scrawled note in his handwriting showed July 1899. What had happened to him in those two years? Katy was determined to help him.

NIGHT ACTION
Alan Evans

Captain David Brent sails at dead of night to the German occupied Normandy town of St. Jean on a mission which will stretch loyalty and ingenuity to its limits, and beyond.

A MURDER TOO MANY
Elizabeth Ferrars

Many, including the murdered man's widow, believed the wrong man had been convicted. The further murder of a key witness in the earlier case convinced Basnett that the seemingly unrelated deaths were linked.

THE WILDERNESS WALK
Sheila Bishop

Stifling unpleasant memories of a misbegotten romance in Cleave with Lord Francis Aubrey, Lavinia goes on holiday there with her sister. The two women are thrust into a romantic intrigue involving none other than Lord Francis.

THE RELUCTANT GUEST
Rosalind Brett

Ann Calvert went to spend a month on a South African farm with Theo Borland and his sister. They both proved to be different from her first idea of them, and there was Storr Peterson — the most disturbing man she had ever met.

ONE ENCHANTED SUMMER
Anne Tedlock Brooks

A tale of mystery and romance and a girl who found both during one enchanted summer.

CLOUD OVER MALVERTON
Nancy Buckingham

Dulcie soon realises that something is seriously wrong at Malverton, and when violence strikes she is horrified to find herself under suspicion of murder.

AFTER THOUGHTS
Max Bygraves

The Cockney entertainer tells stories of his East End childhood, of his RAF days, and his post-war showbusiness successes and friendships with fellow comedians.

MOONLIGHT
AND MARCH ROSES
D. Y. Cameron

Lynn's search to trace a missing girl takes her to Spain, where she meets Clive Hendon. While untangling the situation, she untangles her emotions and decides on her own future.

NURSE ALICE IN LOVE
Theresa Charles

Accepting the post of nurse to little Fernie Sherrod, Alice Everton could not guess at the romance, suspense and danger which lay ahead at the Sherrod's isolated estate.

POIROT INVESTIGATES
Agatha Christie

Two things bind these eleven stories together — the brilliance and uncanny skill of the diminutive Belgian detective, and the stupidity of his Watson-like partner, Captain Hastings.

LET LOOSE THE TIGERS
Josephine Cox

Queenie promised to find the long-lost son of the frail, elderly murderess, Hannah Jason. But her enquiries threatened to unlock the cage where crucial secrets had long been held captive.

THE TWILIGHT MAN
Frank Gruber

Jim Rand lives alone in the California desert awaiting death. Into his hermit existence comes a teenage girl who blows both his past and his brief future wide open.

DOG IN THE DARK
Gerald Hammond

Jim Cunningham breeds and trains gun dogs, and his antagonism towards the devotees of show spaniels earns him many enemies. So when one of them is found murdered, the police are on his doorstep within hours.

THE RED KNIGHT
Geoffrey Moxon

When he finds himself a pawn on the chessboard of international espionage with his family in constant danger, Guy Trent becomes embroiled in moves and countermoves which may mean life or death for Western scientists.

TIGER TIGER
Frank Ryan

A young man involved in drugs is found murdered. This is the first event which will draw Detective Inspector Sandy Woodings into a whirlpool of murder and deceit.

CAROLINE MINUSCULE
Andrew Taylor

Caroline Minuscule, a medieval script, is the first clue to the whereabouts of a cache of diamonds. The search becomes a deadly kind of fairy story in which several murders have an other-worldly quality.

LONG CHAIN OF DEATH
Sarah Wolf

During the Second World War four American teenagers from the same town join the Army together. Forty-two years later, the son of one of the soldiers realises that someone is systematically wiping out the families of the four men.

THE LISTERDALE MYSTERY
Agatha Christie

Twelve short stories ranging from the light-hearted to the macabre, diverse mysteries ingeniously and plausibly contrived and convincingly unravelled.

TO BE LOVED
Lynne Collins

Andrew married the woman he had always loved despite the knowledge that Sarah married him for reasons of her own. So much heartache could have been avoided if only he had known how vital it was to be loved.

ACCUSED NURSE
Jane Converse

Paula found herself accused of a crime which could cost her her job, her nurse's reputation, and even the man she loved, unless the truth came to light.

BUTTERFLY MONTANE
Dorothy Cork

Parma had come to New Guinea to marry Alec Rivers, but she found him completely disinterested and that overbearing Pierce Adams getting entirely the wrong idea about her.

HONOURABLE FRIENDS
Janet Daley

Priscilla Burford is happily married when she meets Junior Environment Minister Alistair Thurston. Inevitably, sexual obsession and political necessity collide.

WANDERING MINSTRELS
Mary Delorme

Stella Wade's career as a concert pianist might have been ruined by the rudeness of a famous conductor, so it seemed to her agent and benefactor. Even Sir Nicholas fails to see the possibilities when John Tallis falls deeply in love with Stella.

CHATEAU OF FLOWERS
Margaret Rome

Alain, Comte de Treville needed a wife to look after him, and Fleur went into marriage on a business basis only, hoping that eventually he would come to trust and care for her.

CRISS-CROSS
Alan Scholefield

As her ex-husband had succeeded in kidnapping their young daughter once, Jane was determined to take her safely back to England. But all too soon Jane is caught up in a new web of intrigue.

DEAD BY MORNING
Dorothy Simpson

Leo Martindale's body was discovered outside the gates of his ancestral home. Is it, as Inspector Thanet begins to suspect, murder?